Feast
FROM THE FIRE

Feast FROM THE FIRE

65 summer recipes to cook and share outdoors

Valerie AIKMAN-SMITH

PHOTOGRAPHY BY ERIN KUNKEL

LONDON • NEW YORK

Designer Geoff Borin
Editor Gillian Haslam
Production Controller David Hearn
Art Director Leslie Harrington
Editorial Director Julia Charles
Publisher Cindy Richards

Food Stylist Valerie-Aikman Smith
Prop Stylist Gena Sigala
Indexer Hilary Bird

First published in 2018 by
Ryland Peters & Small
20–21 Jockey's Fields, London
WC1R 4BW
and
341 E 116th St, New York
NY 10029

www.rylandpeters.com

10 9 8 7 6 5 4 3 2 1

ISBN: 978-1-84975-967-0

Printed in China

A CIP record for this book is available from the British Library.

US Library of Congress Cataloging-in-Publication Data has been
applied for.

Notes:
• American (Imperial plus US cups) and metric measurements
are included in these recipes for your convenience, however it
is important to work with one set of measurements only and not
alternate between the two within a recipe.
• All spoon measurements are level unless otherwise specified.
• All eggs are large (US) and medium (UK), unless specified as
US extra-large, in which case UK large should be used.
• Ovens should be preheated to the specified temperatures. We
recommend using an oven thermometer. If using a fan-assisted
oven, adjust temperatures according to the manufacturer's
instructions.
• When a recipe calls for the grated zest of citrus fruit, buy
unwaxed fruit and wash well before using. If you can only find
treated fruit, scrub well in warm soapy water before using.

CONTENTS

INTRODUCTION 6

FISH & SEAFOOD 10

MEAT & CHICKEN 38

VEGETABLES 68

DESSERTS 100

DRINKS 132

INDEX 158

ACKNOWLEDGMENTS 160

INTRODUCTION

What better way to celebrate summer than to enjoy the very best seasonal food cooked over the fire whether at the beach, when camping, or simply relaxing in your own backyard? Incredible flavors, inspiring ingredients, and the epitome of laid-back entertaining—grilling is the best way to cook in the warmer months and here in this inspirational book you'll discover fish, meat, vegetarian, and vegan recipes to cook and share outdoors.

Combining fresh flavors with exciting grilling techniques, including cooking on a fire pit grill, salt-block cooking, and cedar-plank smoking, chef, food stylist, and author Valerie Aikman-Smith presents 65 recipes perfectly created for relaxed entertaining.

Try delicious fish and seafood recipes including Fish Tacos with Avocado Crema, Spicy Grilled Salmon Collar, Coconut & Lime Shrimp Skewers, and for a special occasion, Grilled Lobster with Flavored Butters. For meat-lovers there's a host of ideas for grilling your favorite fare such as Jerk Pork Chops with Mango Chutney and Grilled Plantains, Smoky Honey Chipotle Ribs, Sriracha & Lime Grilled Chicken Wings, and the crowd-pleasing Lamb Smash Burgers.

Valerie includes fabulous vegetable dishes inspired by market-fresh produce, from Grilled Summer Zucchini with Basil Salt to Roasted Cauliflower & Red Walnut Romesco, plus a refreshing Ouzo Watermelon Salad for those days when the mercury starts to rise.

Effortlessly elegant sweet things designed to round off an alfresco feast include Matcha Ice Cream with Black Sesame Praline, Roasted Strawberry & Ginger Semifreddo, Vin Santo Grilled Peaches, or a classic Grilled Banana Boat.

Finally, if all the heat has made you thirsty, sip on an Apricot & Basil Mimosa and cool down with a Grilled Pineapple Piña Colada, or make up a pitcher of Watermelon Margaritas.

Throughout this book, Valerie draws on her experiences of traveling and cooking in various countries around the world, and shows how simple ingredients can be elevated to a sophisticated level. Whether you are cooking a simple midweek supper in your backyard or preparing an outdoor feast for a special occasion, in these pages you will find the perfect dish to suit your mood.

FISH & SEAFOOD

CEDAR PLANK SALMON
with sake

Wooden planks are a great way to cook fish on the grill as they stop the fish from sticking to the metal grate. I use cedar planks, but there are other varieties of wood that lightly flavor the fish. The wooden planks are soaked in cold water first to prevent them burning over the hot coals.

1 lb/450 g center-cut salmon, skin on

½ cup/125 ml sake

¼ cup/60 ml olive oil, plus extra for drizzling

1 tablespoon wasabi powder

pinch of sea salt

10 shishito peppers, thinly sliced

cracked black pepper

2 lemons, quartered

cedar plank, 7 x 15 inches/ 18 x 38 cm

SERVES 4

Soak the cedar plank in cold water for a minimum of 3 hours, up to a maximum of 24 hours.

Rinse the salmon under cold water and pat dry with paper towels. Place in a ceramic baking dish.

In a small bowl, whisk together the sake, olive oil, wasabi powder, and sea salt. Pour over the salmon and marinate for 20 minutes.

Heat the grill/barbecue to medium–high. Place the wet plank on the grill and leave it there for 6–8 minutes until the wood is charred on one side.

Turn the plank over. Remove the salmon from the marinade and place on top of the charred side of the plank. Sprinkle with the sliced shishito peppers and some cracked black pepper. Close the lid of the grill and cook for 15–20 minutes until the salmon is cooked. Times may differ depending on the thickness of the fish, so check for doneness by inserting a sharp knife into the fish—the flesh should be opaque in the middle.

Serve on the plank with the lemons and drizzle with a little extra olive oil.

Vine–leaf
GRILLED TROUT

Ask your fishmonger to butterfly the fish for you, but if that is not an option you can easily do it yourself. Take a sharp knife and run it along the under-belly of the fish, opening up the cavity. You can also make the stuffing with a variety of vegetables and fruits.

4 whole trout, butterflied

16 brined vine leaves

2 cups/500 g cooked wild rice

1 cup/90 g grapes, roughly chopped, plus 2 bunches of grapes for grilling

small bunch of dill, chopped

¼ cup/60 ml olive oil, plus extra for drizzling

¼ cup/60 ml freshly squeezed lemon juice

sea salt and cracked black pepper

lemon wedges, to serve

oil, for brushing the grate

kitchen twine

SERVES 4

Rinse the fish under cold water and pat dry with paper towels.

Place four vine leaves close together on a work surface and place one trout on top. Repeat with the rest of the fish.

In a bowl mix together the cooked rice, chopped grapes, dill, oil, and lemon juice and season with salt and pepper. Stuff each trout with a quarter of the rice mixture.

Fold the vine leaves around the fish and tie tightly with kitchen twine. Drizzle with a little olive oil and season with salt and pepper.

Heat the grill/barbecue to medium–high. Brush the grate with oil.

Place the bunches of grapes on the grill and cook until the fruit has caramelized and the grapes are beginning to burst open. Set aside on a platter.

Grill the trout for 5 minutes, then use a large spatula to turn them over. Reduce the heat or move the fish to a cooler part of the grill. Cook for another 5–8 minutes until the flesh is white and firm.

Remove the fish from the grill and cut off the twine. Serve with lemon wedges and the caramelized grapes.

BRANZINI

in a salt crust

Deliciously rich in flavor, branzini (also known as European sea bass) are the perfect fish to cook in a salt crust. You can cook any kind of fish in a salt crust and stuff with a variety of herbs and spices—here I have used a stuffing of lemons and lemon leaves which adds a bright, sunny flavor. Serve with a robust green salad and chilled wine.

2 whole branzini

4 lemons, thinly sliced

12 lemon leaves (optional)

2 tablespoons freshly chopped rosemary

½ cup/120 ml white wine

cracked black pepper

8 cups/2 kg coarse sea salt

SERVES 4

Heat the grill/barbecue to medium–high.

Rinse the fish under cold running water. Lay the fish on a work surface and pat dry with paper towels. Divide the lemons and leaves, if using, into four and stuff the cavity of each fish with them. Sprinkle with the rosemary and drizzle with the white wine. Season with pepper.

Pour the salt into a large bowl and add enough cold water to make it the consistency of wet sand, about 2½ cups/625 ml.

Spread half the salt mixture on a baking sheet and lay the fish on top. Cover the fish with the remainder of the salt and pack it tightly, making sure there are no holes for the steam to escape.

Place the baking sheet on top of the grill and close the lid. Bake for 40 minutes, then remove the fish from the grill and rest untouched for 5 minutes.

Using the back of large knife, crack open the salt crust. Remove the salt from around the fish and serve.

Spicy grilled
SALMON COLLAR

Salmon collar is a lesser known cut that was once thrown away or used for bait. You have probably eaten it at your local Japanese restaurant, but now it is popping up in a lot of restaurants as chefs are discovering how wonderful and delicious the meat is. Ask your local fishmonger to source it for you and try this hardy piece of fish on the grill next time you fire it up. This marinade also works well with salmon belly.

4 salmon collars, about 2 lb/ 900 g in total

3 tablespoons sambal oelek

2 tablespoons toasted sesame oil, plus extra for tossing

¼ cup/60 ml mirin

1 tablespoon tamari or soy sauce, plus extra for seasoning

2 tablespoons freshly grated ginger

sea salt and cracked black pepper

1 lb/450 g shishito peppers

black sesame seeds, to garnish (optional)

sweet chilli sauce, to serve (optional)

oil, for brushing the grate

SERVES 4–6

Place the salmon collars in a ceramic baking dish large enough to hold them.

In a medium-sized bowl whisk together the sambal oelek, sesame oil, mirin, tamari, and ginger and season with salt and pepper. Pour the marinade over the fish. Cover and refrigerate for 30 minutes.

Remove the fish from the fridge and bring to room temperature.

Heat the grill/barbecue to medium–high. Brush the grate with oil.

Toss the shishito peppers in a bowl with a splash of sesame oil just to coat. Place on the grill and cook for about 5 minutes, turning once, until they are charred and soft. Remove to a platter, sprinkle with a dash of tamari, and set aside.

Remove the collars from the marinade and place skin-side down on the grill. Cook for 5 minutes, then turn the collars over and lower the heat or move to a cooler part of the grill and continue to cook for another 10 minutes until crispy and just cooked through.

Remove from the grill and place on a platter. Place the shishito peppers alongside and sprinkle with sea salt and sesame seeds, if using. If you wish, serve with sweet chilli sauce.

PAELLA *on the grill*

Paella is one of my favorite dishes to cook over an open fire. Gorgeous dark red tomatoes along with perfumed saffron, mixed with rice and topped with prawns all bubble together. Use good rice such as Bomba, or any rice from Valencia in Spain. Serve with a fine Rioja.

4 tablespoons/60 ml extra virgin olive oil

1 dry-cured Spanish chorizo sausage (about 8 oz/225 g), sliced

4 shallots, finely chopped

2 garlic cloves, finely chopped

1½ teaspoons Spanish smoked paprika

2 teaspoons hot red pepper/chilli flakes

6 medium ripe tomatoes, roughly chopped

1½ cups/375 ml fish stock

1 cup/240 ml white wine

½ teaspoon saffron, soaked in 3 tablespoons warm water

1½ cups/330 g paella rice

20 large shrimp/prawns, shells intact

20 mussels

sea salt and freshly ground black pepper

1 bunch of flat-leaf parsley, chopped, to garnish

lemon wedges, to serve

SERVES 6–8

Heat the grill/barbecue to medium–high.

Place a paella pan or large skillet/frying pan on the grill and add 2 tablespoons of the olive oil. Add the chorizo to the pan and cook for about 2–3 minutes, until the sausage is brown and crispy. Remove from the pan to a plate and set aside.

Add the remaining olive oil, shallots, and garlic and cook for 2 minutes until golden, then add the paprika and hot red pepper/chilli flakes and stir to combine. Tip in the tomatoes and, stirring occasionally, cook for about 5 minutes until they have broken down into a sauce. Season with salt and pepper.

Pour the stock, wine and saffron into a pan and place on the grill. Bring to the boil, then move to a cooler part of the grill to keep at a simmer.

Stir the rice into the tomato mixture and cook for 2 minutes. Pour the hot stock mixture over the rice and stir. Bring to the boil, then move to a cooler part of the grill and simmer for 8–10 minutes without stirring.

Add the shrimp/prawns, mussels, and chorizo and gently push down into the rice. Cover the pan with foil and cook for another 10–15 minutes until the shrimp are cooked through and the mussels have opened up (discard any which have not opened).

Remove the pan from the grill and rest for 5 minutes, then remove the foil. Sprinkle with the parsley and serve with lemon wedges.

GRILLED LOBSTERS
with flavored butters

I love lobsters, and have eaten them since my childhood on the West coast of Scotland where the small wooden fishing boats would bring them into the harbor. They are so easy to throw on the grill and serve up with an array of flavored butters. I steam the lobsters first and then put them on the grill, as this makes the meat juicy and tender.

4 cooked lobsters, about 2 lb/ 900 g each, steamed or boiled

oil, for brushing the grate

sea salt and freshly ground black pepper

good crusty bread, to serve

NORI SEAWEED BUTTER

2 sheets of nori seaweed, crumbled

2 sticks/225 g salted butter

WASABI BUTTER

2 tablespoons wasabi powder

2 sticks/225 g salted butter

GARLIC & CHILI BUTTER

6 garlic cloves, peeled

1 jalapeño, roughly chopped

2 sticks/225 g salted butter

SERVES 4

To make the seaweed butter, place the nori and butter in the bowl of a food processor and pulse until smooth. Season with salt and pepper and spoon into a small bowl. Clean the food processor bowl.

Repeat the process with the wasabi and butter by placing in the food processor and pulse to combine, then season with salt and pepper and spoon into a small bowl.

Lastly, place the garlic, jalapeño, and butter in the food processor. Pulse to combine completely, season with salt and pepper, and spoon into a small bowl.

Heat the grill/barbecue to medium–high. Brush the grate with oil.

Crack the claws and brush the lobsters with olive oil, then season with salt and pepper. Using sharp scissors, cut the underneath of the lobster from top to bottom. Place the lobsters on the grill and cook for 5 minutes, then use tongs to turn them over and continue to cook for another 5 minutes or until the flesh is white and has no translucency.

Serve the lobsters along with the flavored butters and crusty bread.

Garlic chili SHRIMP

At my local farmers' market there is a fisherman from Santa Barbara who sells ridgeback prawns—a small, local, sweet-tasting shrimp/prawn. Sunday night supper is a large cast-iron pan set in the middle of the table with juicy garlic chili prawns to be eaten with your hands and the juices mopped up with crusty rustic bread. You can use any type of shrimp/prawn that has the head and shell intact, simply increase the cooking time slightly for larger ones.

2 lb/900 g shrimp/prawns, heads on

1 whole head of garlic

1 tablespoon hot red pepper/ chilli flakes

¼ cup/60 ml olive oil

2 tablespoons fresh oregano leaves

sea salt and cracked black pepper

good crusty bread, to serve

SERVES 4–6

Place the shrimp/prawns in a large bowl and set aside.

Break the garlic head into cloves, peel, and place in the bowl of a food processor along with the hot red pepper/chilli flakes and olive oil. Process until the garlic is broken into small chunks.

Pour the garlic mixture over the shrimp/prawns and sprinkle with the oregano leaves. Season with salt and pepper and toss to combine. Set aside for 5 minutes.

Heat the grill/barbecue to medium–high.

Place a large cast-iron pan on the grill and heat until just smoking. Place the shrimp/prawns and all the juices in the hot pan and cook for 6–8 minutes, turning every few minutes until they are cooked through. Cook a little longer if the shrimp/prawns are larger.

Serve alongside a basket of crusty bread.

Coconut & lime
SHRIMP SKEWERS

Himalayan salt blocks are so pretty to look at, with strains of pinks marbled through the salt, and are perfect to use as a serving dish for sushi or chilled fruits in summer. You can also cook meat, vegetables, and fish on them as they work really well on a grill. Afterward, simply rinse off under cold water, let dry, and they are ready to use again.

2 lb/900 g peeled shrimp/ prawns, tails on

14-fl oz/400-ml can of unsweetened coconut milk

1 tablespoon curry powder

1 tablespoon ground turmeric

1 tablespoon finely minced fresh ginger

1 teaspoon hot red pepper/ chilli flakes

3 tablespoons fish sauce

½ cup/35 g dried coconut flakes

16 kaffir lime leaves

limes, for squeezing

Himalayan pink salt block

8 wooden skewers, soaked in cold water

SERVES 4

Rinse the shrimp/prawns under cold running water and pat dry with paper towels. Place in a ceramic baking dish.

In a medium-sized bowl, whisk together the coconut milk, curry powder, turmeric, ginger, hot red pepper/chilli flakes, and fish sauce. Pour the marinade over the shrimp/prawns and add the coconut flakes. Toss to make sure they are completely covered. Cover and refrigerate until ready to use.

Place the salt block on a cold grill/barbecue and heat to 400°F (200°C). Once it has reached this temperature, let the salt block continue to heat for another 30 minutes.

While the block is heating, prepare the skewers. Remove the shrimp/prawns from the refrigerator and divide into eight portions. Thread onto the wooden skewers, alternating with the lime leaves. Brush the shrimp/prawns with a little more of the marinade, then discard any remaining.

Place the skewers on the salt block and cook for 4 minutes, then turn them over and continue to cook for another 4 minutes until the centers of the shrimp/prawns are opaque.

Serve with limes for squeezing over.

CLAM STEAMERS
with Calabrian chiles

Serve this with plenty of crusty bread to soak up the wonderful smoky sauce the clams are nestled in. This is a real summer dish for the barbecue, and you can use any kind of clams or mussels and swap out white wine for Madeira wine or beer. The Calabrian chiles bring a pleasantly warm heat to the dish.

¼ cup/60 ml olive oil

2 garlic cloves, finely minced

1 large yellow onion, diced

1 cured chorizo sausage (about 8 oz/225 g), sliced

12 ripe cherry tomatoes

1 bay leaf

½ teaspoon smoked pimento

2 Calabrian chiles/chillies, roughly chopped

3 cups/700 ml dry white wine

30 Little Neck clams, cleaned

sea salt and cracked black pepper

crusty loaf or baguette, to serve

SERVES 4

Heat the grill/barbecue to medium–high.

Place a large cast-iron pan on the grill and pour in the olive oil. Add the garlic and onion and cook for 2–3 minutes. Add the chorizo and continue to cook for another 5 minutes, stirring frequently.

Stir in the tomatoes, bay leaf, pimento, and chiles/chillies and cook for a further 3 minutes.

Pour in the wine and season with the salt and pepper. Bring to the boil and cook for 6–8 minutes until the sauce thickens and the tomatoes are broken down.

Add the clams to the pan. Cover and cook for 6–8 minutes, stirring halfway through, until all the clams have opened. Discard any that stay closed.

Serve in bowls, with bread on the side for mopping up all the juices.

GRILLED PIZZA
with oysters & Parmesan cream

Pizzas are so easy to cook on the grill, and fast too. You don't need a pizza stone or have to preheat the oven. Grilling transforms the dough into a wonderful charred crispy base for your favorite toppings. You can also use readymade pizza dough, if you wish, to make your summer easier.

1¾ cups/220 g all-purpose/plain flour

1½ teaspoons rapid rise yeast (instant yeast)

1 teaspoon sea salt

⅔ cup/160 ml warm water

1 cup/100 g grated Parmesan cheese, plus extra for sprinkling

1 cup/250 ml heavy/double whipping cream

16 medium or 8 large freshly shucked oysters

4 Calabrian chiles/chillies, sliced

fennel pollen, for sprinkling

arugula/rocket leaves

extra virgin olive oil, for oiling the bowl

oil, for brushing the grate

SERVES 2

Oil a large bowl and set aside.

Place the flour, yeast, and salt in the bowl of a food processor. With the motor running, add the water to the flour mixture in a steady stream until all the liquid is incorporated and the dough forms a ball —this takes about 3 minutes.

Place the dough on a floured worktop and knead to form a ball. Place in the oiled bowl and cover with a kitchen towel. Set aside in a warm place for about 3 hours to proof and double in size.

To make the Parmesan cream, place the cheese and cream in a saucepan and bring to the boil. Reduce to a simmer and, stirring continuously, cook until the cheese has melted and you have a sauce. Remove from the heat and set aside.

Heat the grill/barbecue to medium–high. Brush the grate with oil.

Remove the dough from the bowl and cut into 2 pieces. Roll each piece out into a circle about 10 inches/25 cm in diameter.

If your grill/barbecue is big enough, you can cook both pizzas at the same time; if not, cook one at time. Place the dough on the hot grill and cook for 3–5 minutes until golden and charred. Turn the crusts over and liberally spread with the Parmesan cream. Top with the oysters and chiles/chillies and sprinkle with some fennel pollen.

Close the lid and cook for another 5 minutes until the oysters are cooked through and the pizza is charred and crusty.

To serve, remove from the grill onto a wooden board, sprinkle with some grated Parmesan and top with arugula/rocket leaves.

FISH TACOS *with avocado crema*

Tacos are a staple of California living and are our go-to fast food. The streets of LA are full of vendors with small carts selling all kinds of imaginative tacos bursting with grilled meats, fish, vegetables, and cactus and drizzled with exotic hot sauces and cooling cremas. Grill at home and adorn your table with colorful bowls of pickles, sauces, cheeses, and grilled vegetables to pile on to warm tortillas.

1 lb/450 g snapper, tilapia, or cod fillets

1 teaspoon chili powder

1 tablespoon avocado oil or olive oil

zest and freshly squeezed juice of 3 limes

1 avocado, pitted and peeled

1 cup/225 g Mexican crema or crème fraîche

small bunch of cilantro/coriander

12 jalapeños

sea salt and cracked black pepper

12 corn or flour tortillas

oil, for brushing the grate

TO SERVE

lime wedges, radishes, pickled onions, cilantro/coriander, queso fresca, and hot sauces

SERVES 6

Place the fish in a ceramic baking dish. In a small bowl whisk together the chili powder, oil, half the lime zest, and half the juice and pour over the fish. Season with salt and pepper, cover, and set aside for 20 minutes.

Place the avocado, crema, remaining lime zest and juice, and cilantro/coriander in a blender and purée until you have a smooth sauce. Pour into a bowl, season with salt, and set aside.

Heat the grill/barbecue to medium–high. Brush the grate with oil.

Grill the jalapeños for about 4 minutes until blistered and charred, then remove to a serving bowl.

Place the fish on the grill and cook for 3–4 minutes. Using a wide spatula, turn the fish over and cook for another 3–4 minutes until it is cooked through and slightly charred. Cooking times may differ depending on the thickness of the fish. Remove to a warm plate and tent with foil.

Grill the tortillas for a minute on each side until warmed through. Pile in a kitchen towel and wrap to keep them warm.

Flake the fish into large chunks with a fork and place on a platter along with the grilled jalapeños, tortillas, and avocado crema. Serve bowls of radishes, pickled onions, cilantro/coriander, queso fresca, and hot sauces and invite your guests to build their own taco.

POKE *bowls*

Originating in Hawaii where sea fish is at its best, the poké bowl is made with yellowtail or ahi tuna and is served as an appetizer. Now that the poké bowl has traveled outside of the islands, it has taken on a new life. It is popping up with an assortment of vegetables, noodles, pickles, tofu, and all things healthy and fresh. If you are not crazy about raw fish, then grill it for a couple of minutes on each side.

1 lb/450 g very fresh sushi-grade ahi tuna

vegetable oil, if you wish to grill the fish

2 tablespoons toasted sesame oil

2 tablespoons tamari or soy sauce

zest and freshly squeezed juice of 1 lime, plus extra wedges for serving

1 tablespoon mirin

1 jalapeño, finely diced

1 tablespoon finely chopped pickled ginger

sea salt and freshly ground black pepper

2 cups/500 g cooked sushi rice or white rice

6 scallions/spring onions, finely sliced

6 radishes, finely sliced

1 avocado, peeled, pitted, and sliced into wedges

1 Persian cucumber, finely sliced

sesame seeds, for sprinkling

Nori Komi Furikake (Asian seaweed mix)

SERVES 2

Rinse the tuna under cold running water and pat dry with paper towels. Cut the tuna into 1-inch/2.5-cm chunks and place in a bowl. (If you prefer the tuna lightly cooked, grill it for just a few minutes on each side until slightly charred but still pink in the middle, and then cut into chunks.)

In another bowl whisk together the sesame oil, tamari, lime zest and juice, mirin, jalapeño, and ginger. Season to taste, pour over the tuna, and toss to combine.

Divide the rice between two serving bowls and top with the tuna, scallions/spring onions, radishes, avocado, and cucumber. Drizzle with some of the dressing and sprinkle with sesame seeds and Nori Komi Furikake.

Serve with lime wedges to squeeze.

MEAT & CHICKEN

Sriracha & lime grilled
CHICKEN WINGS

I have a Kaffir lime tree in my garden and use the fruit and leaves to perfume and flavor dishes all the time. You can also use regular lime juice and leaves in this dish to add a pleasant, cooling contrast to all the spices. Chicken wings are fun appetizer to hand around or to take to the beach for a picnic.

24 chicken wings

¼ cup/60 ml sriracha

¼ cup/60ml sambal oelek

¾ cup/180 ml dark runny honey, such as avocado

½ cup/125 ml toasted sesame oil

4 garlic cloves

2 kaffir limes, or regular limes, quartered

6 kaffir lime leaves, or regular lime leaves, shredded

1 small onion, roughly chopped

sea salt and cracked black pepper

1 tablespoon black sesame seeds

tangerine wedges, to serve

oil, for brushing the grate

SERVES 4–6

Rinse the chicken wings under running cold water and pat dry with paper towels. Place in a large ceramic dish or bowl.

Place the sriracha, sambal oelek, honey, sesame oil, garlic, lime quarters, lime leaves, and onion in a blender and process until you have a smooth sauce. Season with salt and pepper. Pour the sauce over the chicken wings and toss to coat. Cover and refrigerate for 4 hours or overnight.

When you are ready to cook, remove the chicken wings from the fridge and bring to room temperature.

Heat the grill/barbecue to medium–high. Brush the grate with oil.

Cook the wings on the grill for 6–8 minutes, then turn them over and either turn the heat down or move to a cooler part of the grill. Continue to cook for a further 8 minutes, turning occasionally to make sure they are cooked through and crispy on the outside.

Place the cooked wings on a large plate and sprinkle with the sesame seeds. Serve with the tangerine wedges.

Grilled *harissa* CHICKEN KABOBS

This is one of my all-time favorite dishes to grill—spicy chicken, hot off the grill and served with lemon wedges and cracked green olives is divine. Serve with ice-cold beers and relax. Store the extra harissa in the fridge and use it to flavor stews, pastas, or grilled vegetables and to spoon through rice dishes.

12 chicken thighs, skin on, boneless

¼ cup/60 ml honey

1 cup/225 g scratched green olives

lemon wedges, for squeezing

oil, for brushing the grate

FOR THE HARISSA

2 dried Pasilla chiles/chillies

1 dried Ancho chile/chilli

1 roasted red (bell) pepper

2 fresh red Serrano chiles/ chillies, roughly chopped

2 teaspoons ground cumin

2 tablespoons tomato paste/ tomato purée

1 teaspoon smoked paprika

4 garlic cloves, peeled and bashed

2 tablespoons olive oil

½ teaspoon kosher salt

SERVES 6–8

To make the harissa, place the dried chiles/chillies in a bowl, cover with boiling water, and soak for 30 minutes. Drain the chiles, reserving a ¼ cup/60 ml of the soaking liquid.

Place the chiles, reserved liquid, and the remaining harissa ingredients in a blender and blend until you have a rough paste.

Place the chicken thighs in a large ceramic dish. Mix together 4 tablespoons of the harissa paste with the honey. Pour over the chicken and toss to coat completely. Cover and refrigerate for 6–24 hours. (Pour the remaining harissa into a jar with a tight-fitting lid and refrigerate for up to 6 months.)

Remove the chicken from the fridge and thread onto metal skewers. Bring to room temperature.

Heat the grill/barbecue to medium–high. Brush the grate with oil.

Place the skewers skin-side down on the grill and cook for 8 minutes until golden brown and crispy. Turn the skewers over and turn down the heat or move to a cooler part of the grill. Continue to cook for another 15 minutes. Check for doneness by inserting a sharp knife into the chicken to see that the meat is no longer pink and the juices run clear.

Remove the cooked skewers from the grill, cover, and rest for 5 minutes. To serve, pile on a plate and sprinkle with the olives and lemon wedges (if you wish, the lemon wedges can be briefly charred on the grill).

Cajun FRIED CHICKEN

Fried chicken is a real summer dish especially suited to those long sunny days spent at the beach. Wrap it up for a picnic as it's as delicious eaten cold as hot. Generously sprinkle with lemon zest and sea salt for that extra tang and serve with an array of hot sauces.

4 lb/2 kg chicken, cut into 10 pieces

1½ cups/375 ml buttermilk

1 egg

1 cup/130 g all-purpose/ plain flour

½ cup/75 g cornmeal/polenta

6 cups/1.4 litres vegetable oil, for deep frying

sea salt, for sprinkling

lemon zest, for sprinkling

lemon wedges, for squeezing

FOR THE CAJUN SEASONING

2 teaspoons cumin

2 teaspoons cayenne

2 tablespoons Spanish smoked paprika

2 teaspoons dried oregano

1 teaspoon dried garlic powder

1 teaspoon sea salt

1 teaspoon freshly ground black pepper

SERVES 4–6

To make the Cajun seasoning, mix all the ingredients together in a small bowl.

Place the chicken pieces in a large ceramic baking dish. In a bowl whisk together the buttermilk, egg, and 2 tablespoons of the Cajun seasoning. Pour over the chicken, making sure the pieces are evenly coated. Cover and refrigerate for 4–24 hours.

In a shallow bowl mix together the flour, cornmeal/polenta, and 1 tablespoon of the Cajun seasoning. (Store the remaining seasoning in an airtight container.)

Remove the chicken from the fridge and bring to room temperature.

Pour the oil into a 5-quart/5-litre Dutch oven or deep-fat fryer and heat until it registers 375°F/190°C on a deep-frying thermometer.

Remove the chicken from the buttermilk and shake off any excess marinade. Dredge each piece in the flour mix and, working in batches, fry the chicken in the hot oil for 8–10 minutes. Cook until dark golden brown and cooked through.

Remove the chicken pieces from the oil, drain on paper towels, and sprinkle with the sea salt and lemon zest. Serve with lemon wedges and store-bought hot sauces.

Piri Piri CORNISH GAME HENS
with citrus-honey dipping sauce

If you can't find Cornish game hens, you can use poussin and if you are not sure about butterflying the birds, ask you butcher to do it for you. Serve these hot off the grill with a cooling citrus-honey sauce and a large crispy green salad.

2 Cornish game hens or poussins

6 hot red chiles/chillies, roughly chopped

2 teaspoons smoked paprika

4 garlic cloves, roughly chopped

zest and freshly squeezed juice of 1 lemon

½ cup/125 ml olive oil

sea salt and freshly ground black pepper

oil, for brushing the grate

FOR THE DIPPING SAUCE

zest and freshly squeezed juice of 2 tangerines

2 tablespoons cider vinegar

2 tablespoons toasted sesame oil

2 tablespoons honey

1 teaspoon mirin

1 teaspoon fish sauce

½ Serrano chile/chilli, thinly sliced

SERVES 4

To butterfly the hens, lay them breast-side down on a worktop and using sharp scissors, cut down each side of the backbone. Discard the backbone. Open the hens up like a book and lay skin-side up in a ceramic dish.

Place the chiles/chillies, paprika, garlic, lemon zest and juice, and olive oil in a blender. Process until smooth and season with salt and pepper. Pour over the hens and place in the fridge uncovered for 6–24 hours (leaving them uncovered gives a crispier chicken skin).

To make the citrus-honey dipping sauce, whisk together all the ingredients in a small bowl. Cover and refrigerate until ready to use.

Heat the grill/barbecue to medium–high. Brush the grate with oil.

Remove the hens from the fridge and bring to room temperature.

Place the hens skin-side down on the grill and cook for about 8–10 minutes until golden brown. Turn the hens over and turn down the heat or move to a cooler part of the grill. Continue to cook for another 20 minutes. Check for doneness by inserting a knife to see that the meat is no longer pink and the juices run clear.

Remove the cooked hens from the grill to a chopping block, tent with foil, and rest for 5 minutes. To serve, cut the hens up and serve with the chilled citrus-honey dipping sauce.

JERK PORK CHOPS
with mango salsa & grilled plantains

A medley of flavors play out here, hot and spicy contrasting with cooling fruits. Grilled plantains are a mainstay of Caribbean cooking and are sweet and delicious. Serve with plain rice and ice-cold beers.

4 bone-in pork chops

4 Habanero or Scotch Bonnet chiles/chillies

2-inch/5-cm piece of fresh ginger, peeled and roughly chopped

4 garlic cloves, peeled and smashed

1 tablespoon ground cinnamon

1 tablespoon ground allspice

1 tablespoon ground nutmeg

3 tablespoons molasses

good pinch of sea salt

oil, for brushing the grate

FOR THE MANGO SALSA

1 large fresh mango, peeled, pitted, and diced

1 shallot, finely minced

1 jalapeño, finely diced

1 small bunch of cilantro/coriander leaves, chopped

zest and freshly squeezed juice of 1 large lime

2 tablespoons olive oil

FOR THE PLANTAINS

4 plantains, peeled and cut in half lengthwise

2 tablespoons olive oil

4 tablespoons honey

SERVES 4

Place the pork chops in a ceramic dish large enough for them to lie in a single layer.

Place the chiles/chillies, ginger, garlic, cinnamon, allspice, nutmeg, molasses, and salt in a blender and process to a coarse purée. Pour the marinade over the pork and toss to make sure the meat is completely covered. Cover and refrigerate for 6–24 hours.

To make the salsa, mix the mango, shallot, jalapeño, cilantro/coriander, lime zest and juice, and oil in a bowl. Cover and refrigerate until ready to use.

Remove the pork from the fridge and bring to room temperature.

Lay the plantains in a ceramic dish. Whisk together the oil and honey and pour over the plantains, making sure they are completely coated. Cover and set aside.

Heat the grill/barbecue to medium–high. Brush the grate with oil.

Grill the pork chops for 6 minutes, then turn over. Reduce the heat slightly or move them to a cooler part of the grill and continue to cook for another 6–8 minutes. To check doneness, insert a sharp knife into the center of the chop—the juices should run clear and the meat be slightly pink. Remove to a plate, cover with foil, and rest for 10 minutes.

Place the plantains on the grill and cook for about 3–4 minutes on each side until dark golden brown and charred. Remove from the grill and serve with the pork chops and chilled mango salsa.

Smoky honey CHIPOTLE RIBS

Everyone loves ribs and baby-back pork ribs can take on powerful smoky flavor and spices. I like to marinate them overnight and have even done it for 48 hours to make sure all the flavors soak into the meat. The ribs should cook over a low indirect heat for as long as possible to ensure the meat is tender and falling off the bones.

2 racks of baby-back pork ribs, membrane removed

1 cup/225 g fig jam

1 cup/240 ml dark honey

7-oz/198-g can of chipotle chiles/chillies in adobo sauce

1 Habanero chile/chilli

1 yellow onion, peeled and roughly chopped

4 garlic cloves, peeled and bashed

3-inch/7.5-cm piece of fresh ginger, peeled and roughly chopped

1 lime, quartered

1½ cups/75 g cilantro/ coriander, roughly chopped

1 teaspoon sea salt

½ teaspoon freshly ground black pepper

oil, for brushing the grate

SERVES 6–8

Place the ribs in a baking dish large enough to hold them in one layer. Place all the remaining ingredients in a blender and process until you have a smooth sauce. Pour the sauce over the ribs, making sure they are completely coated. Cover and refrigerate for 6–24 hours.

When you are ready to cook, remove the ribs from the fridge and bring to room temperature.

Prepare a grill/barbecue for medium–low indirect heat (325–350°F/ 160–180°C)—this means lighting one side of the grill only. Brush the grate with oil. Place a small disposable foil pan filled with water over the heat—this will keep the ribs moist while cooking.

Using tongs, remove the ribs from the marinade and shake off any excess sauce. Reserve the leftover marinade for basting. Lay the ribs meat-side down on the grate away from the heat and close the lid. Cook for 1 hour.

After the first hour, turn the ribs over and baste with the reserved marinade sauce. Replenish the water in the foil pan and close the lid. Cook for another hour.

Baste the ribs one more time and close the lid for another 15 minutes.

Move the ribs over to the directly heated side of the grill and cook for 5 minutes, then turn the ribs over for another 5 minutes until browned and slightly charred.

Remove the ribs to a large wooden board and tent with foil. Rest for 10 minutes, then cut up and serve.

Crispy pork belly
BLUE CORN TACOS

These are the most delicious tacos imaginable—slivers of crispy grilled pork belly wrapped in a blue corn tortilla and topped with an array of veggies. Hit it with freshly squeezed lime and hot sauce and enjoy with a frosty beer. If you can't find blue corn tortillas, use corn or flour.

2 lb/900 g pork belly, skin off

2 bay leaves

¼ cup/60 ml white wine

1 teaspoon sea salt

1 teaspoon black peppercorns

7-oz/198-g can of chipotle peppers in adobo sauce

12 blue corn tortillas or yellow corn

oil, for brushing the grate

TO SERVE

lime wedges, lettuce, tomatoes, radishes, onions, cilantro/coriander, queso fresco, and hot sauces

SERVES 6

Place the pork in a lidded pan and add the bay leaves, white wine, salt, and peppercorns. Pour in enough cold water (about 2 quarts/ 2 litres) to cover the pork by 2 inches/5 cm. Cover and bring to the boil over a medium–high heat, then reduce the heat and let the pork simmer for 1½ hours.

Place the chipotle peppers along with the sauce in a bowl and mash with a fork. Set aside.

Remove the pork from the pan and place on a cutting board. Cover and let it rest and cool for 10 minutes.

Heat the grill/barbecue to medium–high. Brush the grate with oil.

Slice the pork 1½ inches/4 cm thick. Using a pastry brush, coat both sides of the pork slices with a little of the chipotle mix.

Place the pork on the grill and cook for 2 minutes. Using tongs, turn the slices over and cook for another 2–3 minutes until crispy and slightly charred. Remove and place on a large platter.

Place the tortillas on the grill and cook for a minute on each side. Remove to a plate.

Prepare the lime wedges, toppings, and hot sauces and have your guests build their own tacos.

KOREAN GRILLED SKIRT STEAK
with peanut noodles

Beautifully charred on the outside and ruby-red rare inside is how this steak comes off the hot coals. Sliced and nestled on top of peanut noodles, it's the perfect food for summer. I make quick cucumber pickles (see page 66) to go alongside, and also pickle a few green tomatoes too.

1 skirt steak, approx. 2 lb/900 g

Spicy Peanut Noodles (see page 70)

Homemade Pickles (see page 66), to serve

store-bought kimchi, to serve

oil, for brushing the grate

FOR THE MARINADE

⅓ cup/90 ml vegetable oil

⅓ cup/90 ml soy sauce

⅓ cup/90 ml toasted sesame oil

⅓ cup/90 ml honey

3 tablespoons sherry

3 tablespoons curry powder

2 tablespoons freshly grated ginger

4 garlic cloves

sea salt and cracked black pepper

SERVES 4

To make the marinade, place the vegetable oil, soy sauce, sesame oil, honey, sherry, curry powder, ginger, and garlic in a blender and process to a smooth sauce. Season with salt and pepper.

Place the steak in a ceramic baking dish. Pour the marinade over the steak, turning the meat to make sure it is completely covered. Cover and refrigerate for 8–24 hours.

When you are ready to cook, remove the steak from the fridge and bring to room temperature.

Heat the grill/barbecue to medium–high. Brush the grate with oil.

Place the steak on the grill and cook for 5 minutes, then turn the steak over and cook for a further 5 minutes for medium rare. Allow a longer time if you prefer the steak medium to well done.

Remove the steak from the grill, cover, and rest for 10 minutes.

Slice the steak against the grain and serve with the Spicy Peanut Noodles. Serve pickles and kimchi alongside.

GRILLED STEAKS
with grilled tomatillo salsa verde

Here I have used New York strip steaks as this is a cut that grills really well, but you can use any type of steak, bone in or boneless. Scorched and charred tomatillos make a wonderful salsa verde. Slice the steaks up on a big wooden board, generously spoon over the salsa verde, and serve with a big green crispy salad.

6 New York strip/sirloin steaks

½ cup/120 ml olive oil

2 teaspoons smoked sea salt

2 teaspoons ground black pepper

2 teaspoons chipotle chili/chilli powder

4 garlic cloves, finely minced

oil, for brushing the grate

FOR THE SALSA VERDE

12 tomatillos, husks removed

1 yellow onion, cut into quarters

2 Serrano chiles/chillies

2 garlic cloves

small bunch of cilantro/coriander

freshly squeezed juice of 1 lime

salt and freshly ground black pepper

SERVES 6–8

Place the steaks in a ceramic baking dish. In a small bowl, whisk together the oil, salt, pepper, chili/chilli powder, and garlic. Pour over the steaks, making sure both sides are coated. Cover and set aside.

Heat the grill/barbecue to medium–high. Brush the grate with oil.

To make the salsa verde, grill the tomatillos, onion, chiles/chillies, and garlic for about 5–6 minutes until they are cooked through and slightly charred. Transfer the vegetables to a blender, add the cilantro/coriander and lime juice, and process until you have a chunky sauce. Season with salt and pepper, pour into a bowl, and set aside.

Place the steaks on the grill and cook for 5 minutes, then turn them over and cook for a further 5 minutes for medium-rare. Allow a longer time if you prefer your steak medium to well done.

Remove the steaks from the grill to a wooden board, cover with foil, and rest for 10 minutes.

To serve, slice the steaks against the grain and spoon over the salsa verde.

GRILLED LAMB
with North African spices & dates

An explosion of wonderful spices laced with date molasses turns these lamb chops into one of the best things to come off a hot grill. As the dates cook on the hot fire, they caramelize and sweeten to a deep earthy taste. Served with an aromatic creamy hummus, it is perfect for long summer evenings with friends gathered around the grill.

2 racks of lamb

1 tablespoon ground cardamom

1 tablespoon ground cumin

2 teaspoons chili/chilli powder

1 teaspoon ground cloves

1 teaspoon ground cinnamon

1 teaspoon ground allspice

1 teaspoon kosher salt

½ cup/120 ml date molasses

¼ cup/60 ml extra virgin olive oil

24 large dates, pitted/stoned

oil, for brushing the grate

FOR THE HUMMUS

15-oz/440-g can of chickpeas, drained

2 tablespoons tahini

zest and freshly squeezed juice of 1 lemon

2 garlic cloves, peeled and bashed

¼ cup/60 ml extra virgin olive oil

salt and freshly ground black pepper

sumac, for sprinkling

SERVES 4

Cut the lamb racks into single chops and place in a ceramic dish large enough to hold them.

In a bowl mix together the cardamom, cumin, chili/chilli powder, cloves, cinnamon, allspice, salt, date molasses, and olive oil. Pour over the lamb, making sure all the chops are completely covered. Cover and refrigerate for 4–24 hours.

Set aside 2 tablespoons of the chickpeas. Place the remainder of the chickpeas in the bowl of a food processor with the tahini, lemon zest and juice, garlic, and olive oil and pulse until smooth. Season with salt and pepper. Pour the hummus into a bowl, cover, and refrigerate.

Remove the lamb from the fridge and bring to room temperature.

Thread the dates onto skewers and set aside.

Remove the hummus from the fridge and top with the remaining chickpeas. Drizzle with olive oil and sprinkle with a little sumac.

Heat the grill/barbecue to medium–high. Brush the grate with oil.

Place the lamb chops on the grill and cook for 3–4 minutes. Using a pair of tongs, turn the chops over and continue to cook for another 3–4 minutes, or for longer if you prefer your meat well done. Remove the chops to a platter and tent with foil. Rest for 10 minutes.

Place the skewered dates on the grill and cook for 2–3 minutes until caramelized and slightly charred. Serve the chops with the dates and the hummus.

Lamb SMASH BURGERS

Smash burgers are—as the name implies—smashed burgers! The key to success is to cook them in a searing hot cast-iron pan and press the meat down into a flat patty, cooking until they have a crisp crust, then flip them over.

1½ lb/680 g freshly ground/ minced lamb

1 tablespoon dried mint

1 tablespoon dried oregano

1 teaspoon pressed garlic

sea salt and cracked black pepper

4 brioche burger buns or bread of your choice

4 thick tomato slices

crumbled feta cheese, to serve

oil, for brushing the grate

FOR THE AIOLI

2 egg yolks

1 garlic clove

½ teaspoon Dijon mustard

2 tablespoons freshly squeezed lemon juice

1 cup/240 ml extra virgin olive oil

1 cup/225 g Kalamata olives, pitted/stoned and finely chopped

SERVES 4

Place the lamb, mint, oregano, and garlic in a large bowl, season with salt and pepper, then stir to combine.

Divide the mixture into four and form into loose balls. Don't squeeze too hard as you want the mixture to be loose to easily smash down during cooking. Cover and set aside.

To make the aïoli, combine the egg yolks, garlic, mustard, and lemon juice in a food processor and process until smooth. With the motor running, slowly add in the olive oil a few drops at a time. As the mixture thickens, continue to add the oil in a slow, steady stream until it is all combined. Pour into a bowl and stir in the chopped Kalamata olives.

Heat the grill/barbecue to medium–high. Brush the grate with oil.

Place a cast-iron pan or flat-top griddle on top and heat until smoking. Place the burgers in the hot pan and firmly smash down with a flat spatula until they are ½ inch/1 cm thick.

Cook for about 2 minutes until a crisp crust forms. Flip them over and continue to cook for another minute for medium-rare, or longer for well done.

Slice and toast the buns on the grill, then spread the top and bottom with a thick layer of aïoli. Place a burger on the bun base, then top with tomato slices and sprinkle with feta cheese.

PROSCIUTTO & FIG
grilled flatbreads

Flatbreads are such a fun way to start a party. They are quick to cook on the grill and guests can nibble on them while the rest of the meal comes together. One of my favorite combinations is figs and prosciutto, as I love the sweet and salty flavors together. Pick up some flatbreads from your local store if you want to reduce the prep time.

1¾ cups/220 g all-purpose/plain flour

1½ teaspoons rapid-rise yeast (instant yeast)

1 teaspoon sea salt

⅔ cups/160 ml warm water

2 balls of burrata cheese, torn into small pieces

12 slices of prosciutto

6 figs, quartered

4 red Serrano chiles/chillies, sliced

truffle honey, for drizzling

oil, for brushing the grate

MAKES 6 SMALL
FLATBREADS

Oil a large bowl and set aside.

Place the flour, yeast, and salt in the bowl of a food processor. With the motor running, add the warm water to the flour mixture in a steady stream until all the liquid is incorporated and the dough forms a ball —this will take about 3 minutes.

Place the dough on a floured worktop and knead to form a ball. Place in the oiled bowl and cover with a kitchen towel. Set aside in a warm place for about 3 hours to proof and double in size.

Heat the grill/barbecue to medium–high. Brush the grate with oil.

Remove the dough from the bowl and cut into six pieces. Roll each piece out into a circle.

Place the dough on the hot grill and cook for about 3–5 minutes until golden and charred. Using a pair of tongs, turn the flatbreads over. Top each crust with some burrata, two slices of prosciutto, and four pieces of fig. Sprinkle with the Serrano chiles/chillies.

Close the lid and cook for another 5 minutes, until the cheese has melted, the prosciutto is crispy, and the flatbreads are charred and crusty.

To serve, remove from the grill to a wooden board and drizzle with a little truffle honey.

CLASSIC CHEESEBURGER
with homemade pickles

A weekend BBQ is not complete without a classic hamburger. Use high-quality beef that has a good amount of fat in it—that way you will end up with a juicy mouthwatering burger. Homemade pickles add a nice tart crunch. Serve with a large platter piled high with lettuce, tomatoes, and onions and your guests can build their own burger.

1½ lb/680 g freshly ground beef, 20% fat

kosher salt and freshly ground black pepper

4 slices of Cheddar cheese

4 hamburger buns

oil, for brushing the grate

FOR THE PICKLES

6 Persian cucumbers, sliced into rounds

2 bay leaves

2 cups/500 ml white wine vinegar

½ cup/110 g white sugar

2 tablespoons kosher salt

2 teaspoons mustard seeds

TO SERVE

lettuce, sliced onions, ketchup, mayo, tomatoes, pickled chiles/chillies

SERVES 4

Make the pickles ahead of time as they will need to marinate for at least an hour.

Pack the cucumbers and bay leaves into a sterilized glass jar. Bring the vinegar, sugar, salt, mustard seeds, and ¼ cup/60 ml water to the boil in a saucepan over a medium–high heat. Reduce to a simmer and cook for 5 minutes until the sugar has dissolved. Pour the hot mixture over the cucumbers, cap with a tight-fitting lid, and set aside. These will keep for up to 6 months in the fridge.

Place the beef in a bowl, season with salt and pepper, and mix to combine. Gently shape the meat into four patties about 1 inch/2.5 cm thick. Using your thumb, gently make a small indentation in the center of each patty. This ensures they will keep their shape when cooking.

Heat a grill/barbecue to medium–high. Brush the grate with oil.

Place the patties on the grill and cook for 5 minutes. Flip them over and continue to cook for another 5 minutes for medium-rare, or longer for well done. For the last 2 minutes of cooking, place a slice of cheese on top of each patty to melt.

Slice and toast the buns on the grill, then serve alongside the patties, pickles, and platter of fixings.

VEGETABLES

Spicy PEANUT NOODLES

These noodles are cloaked in a wonderful spicy peanut sauce which can be served either ice cold or warm. They make a great summer dish on their own, but are even better served with something caramelized and charred, hot off the grill. Keep the leftover sauce in a glass jar with a lid in the fridge and add a spoonful to dressings or mix into rice.

9-oz/250-g packet of buckwheat soba noodles

⅓ cup/80 g **Doenjang (Korean bean paste)**

⅓ cup/80 g **Gochujang (Korean chili paste)**

cilantro/coriander, chopped, to garnish

sesame seeds, to garnish

4 limes, quartered

Cucumber Pickles (see page 66)

FOR THE SAUCE

2 tablespoons dark honey

2 tablespoons toasted sesame oil

½ yellow onion, roughly chopped

3 scallions/spring onions, roughly chopped

2 tablespoons peanut butter

2 tablespoons rice wine vinegar

salt and freshly ground black pepper

SERVES 4
SAUCE YIELDS 1 CUP/250 ML

Cook the soba noodles according to the packet instructions. Rinse under cold water and set aside.

To make the sauce, place the honey, sesame oil, onion, scallions/spring onions, peanut butter, and vinegar in a blender and process until smooth. Season with salt and pepper.

Place the noodles in a large bowl and spoon over 2–3 tablespoons of the sauce. Toss together, making sure the noodles are well coated in the sauce. Sprinkle with cilantro/coriander and sesame seeds. Serve the limes on the side for squeezing over, along with the Cucumber Pickles.

Charred Treviso SALAD

Charred Treviso bathed in an anchovy and almond dressing is a delicious accompaniment to any cookout. It's a hardy but milder relative of radicchio and has pretty, long leaves that are tinged with green and white. The anchovy and breadcrumbs add sweetness to this salad.

½ cup/55 g almonds, roughly chopped

2-oz/56-g can of anchovies

2 cups/100 g panko breadcrumbs

3 tablespoons salted capers

¼ cup/60 ml olive oil

4 small Treviso chicory/radicchio, cut in half lengthwise

¼ cup/30g grated Parmesan cheese (optional)

cracked black pepper

oil, for brushing the grate

SERVES 6–8

Place the almonds and anchovies (there's no need to drain them) in a food processor and pulse to a rough consistency. Pour the mixture into a bowl and add the breadcrumbs, capers, and half the olive oil. Toss together and season with pepper.

Heat a pan over a medium–high heat, add the breadcrumb mixture, and toast until golden brown. Set aside.

Heat the grill/barbecue to medium–high. Brush the grate with oil.

Place the Treviso on a baking sheet and brush with the remaining olive oil. Grill for 2–3 minutes on each side until slightly charred and wilted.

Remove them to a platter and scatter with the breadcrumb mix. Sprinkle with the Parmesan, if using, and season with a little more black pepper.

Ouzo watermelon SALAD

Serve this refreshingly simple, eye-catching salad when the mercury starts to rise. The ouzo infuses the watermelon just a little, enhancing all that sweet goodness. It's the perfect salad to pack up and take to the beach to enjoy while watching the sun set.

1 watermelon

½ cup/120 ml ouzo

4 Persian cucumbers

1 lb/450 g feta cheese, crumbled

1 cup/130 g pitted/stoned Kalamata olives

¼ cup/60 ml extra virgin olive oil

small bunch of oregano

sea salt and cracked black pepper

SERVES 6

Place the watermelon on a work surface and cut into quarters. Remove the skin, cut the flesh into 1½-inch/4-cm cubes, and place in a large bowl.

Pour the ouzo over the watermelon and gently toss together to make sure all the pieces are coated. Marinate for 20 minutes.

Chop the cucumber into 1½-inch/4-cm chunks and add to the watermelon. Add the feta and olives and pour over the olive oil. Season with salt and pepper and gently toss to combine.

Serve on a large platter and scatter with oregano leaves.

GRILLED AVOCADOS
with Mescal & lime dressing

Avocados trees grow all over California and their fruits are a big part of everyday meals. Grilling them deepens the flavor, while dousing them in a perfumed Mescal and lime dressing is divine. Next time you make guacamole, try charring the avocados on the grill before mashing them.

4 avocados

¼ cup/60 ml orange blossom honey

¼ cup/60 ml extra virgin olive oil

¼ cup/60ml Mescal

zest and freshly squeezed juice of 2 large limes

sea salt and cracked black pepper

oil, for brushing the grate

SERVES 6

Halve the avocados and remove the pits/stones. Leave the skin on.

In a small bowl whisk together the honey, oil, Mescal, and lime zest and juice. Season with salt and pepper and set aside.

Heat the grill/barbecue to medium–high. Brush the grate with oil.

Place the avocados cut-side down on the grill and cook for about 3–4 minutes until slightly charred and browned. Turn them over and cook for another 2 minutes.

Remove from the grill and place on a platter, drizzle with the Mescal and lime dressing, and serve.

Roasted
STUFFED TOMATOES

Roasted tomatoes are one of the highlights of summer cooking, especially if you choose heirloom varieties for their kaleidoscope of colors and rich taste. After cooking on the grill, drizzle the tomatoes with aromatic pesto sauce for a melt-in-your-mouth delight.

6 large heirloom tomatoes

½ cup/100 g pitted/stoned Kalamata olives, roughly chopped

1 cup/135 g feta cheese, crumbled

2 tablespoons oregano leaves

½ cup/115 g Pesto Sauce (see page 94)

sea salt and cracked black pepper

olive oil, for drizzling

SERVES 6

Heat the grill/barbecue to medium–high.

Place the tomatoes on a work surface. Using a serrated knife, slice the tops off and set aside.

Using a teaspoon, scoop out the insides of the tomatoes and place the pulp in a medium-sized bowl. Add the olives, feta, and oregano and stir to combine. Season with salt and pepper—you will only need a touch of salt as the feta is a salty cheese.

Place the tomatoes in a snug-fitting baking dish. Stuff each tomato with the feta cheese mixture and place the tomato tops back on. Drizzle with olive oil.

Place the baking dish on the grate of the barbecue and close the lid. Cook for 10 minutes, then check them. You may need to either reduce the heat or move them to a cooler part of the grill. Continue to cook until the tomatoes are soft but are still keeping their shape.

When ready, remove the tomatoes from the grill, drizzle with a little pesto, and serve.

Jicama, APPLE & FENNEL SLAW

Jicama is a wonderful bulbous vegetable commonly found in Mexican cooking. It has a crisp texture, similar to an apple, and is eaten raw in fresh summer and winter slaws or as a crudité. Yuzu is a sour Japanese citrus fruit, which is a bit like a cross between an orange and lime. It can be a little hard to find fresh but you can source bottled yuzu on the internet or from Asian stores. It is a useful pantry staple, to be used in dressings, drizzled over ceviche, or splashed into a weekend cocktail. You can substitute it with grapefruit or lime juice.

1 small jicama
4 red beets/beetroots
4 golden beets/beetroots
1 fennel bulb
1 Poblano chile/chilli
¼ cup/60 ml bottled
yuzu juice
2 tablespoons ponzu sauce
3 tablespoons mirin
2 tablespoons maple syrup
zest and freshly squeezed
juice of 1 lime
small bunch of marjoram

SERVES 6

Peel the jicama and beets/beetroot and set aside.

Using a mandolin, one by one shred the jicama, beets, fennel, and poblano chile/chilli and place in a large bowl.

Whisk together the yuzu, ponzu, mirin, maple syrup, and lime zest and juice. Pour over the slaw and toss to combine. Cover and refrigerate for about 30 minutes, to allow the flavors to meld together.

Tip out onto a large platter, sprinkle with marjoram leaves, and serve chilled.

GRILLED HEIRLOOM

gazpacho cups

Grilling the tomatoes, peppers, chiles/chillies, and garlic gives
a wonderfully deep smoky and sweet flavor to this gazpacho.
I like to serve it in cups as this makes a fun way to start a party.
Use good Spanish sherry vinegar from Jerez de La Frontera to flavor.

**12 ripe but firm heirloom
tomatoes**

2 garlic cloves, unpeeled

**1 yellow onion, cut in half,
unpeeled**

1 red (bell) pepper

**2 Serrano chiles/chillies, red
or green**

**2 Persian cucumbers, roughly
chopped**

**¼ cup/60 ml extra virgin olive
oil, plus extra for drizzling**

**¼ cup/60 ml Jerez sherry
vinegar**

**sea salt and cracked black
pepper**

**tomato flowers or herbs, to
garnish (optional)**

oil, for brushing the grate

SERVES 6–8

Heat the grill/barbecue to medium–high. Brush the grate with oil.

Place the tomatoes, garlic, onion, pepper, and chiles/chillies on
the grill and cook, turning often, until charred and softened but still
keeping their shape.

Remove the vegetables from the grill and place on a cutting board.
Peel the onions and garlic and cut off the ends.

Place all the grilled vegetables and the cucumbers in a blender
along with the olive oil and vinegar and process until you have a
slightly chunky soup. Season with salt and pepper and chill in the
fridge for 2–24 hours.

Fill cups with the chilled gazpacho, drizzle with a little olive oil, and
garnish with tomato flowers or herbs, if using.

GRILLED SUMMER ZUCCHINI
with basil salt

Bright yellow squash blossoms are so beautiful and delicious at the same time. They shout out summer in all its glory, just as daffodils announce springtime. Grilling the zucchini/courgettes and their flowers on hot coals, then sprinkling with basil salt is simple and perfect for any occasion.

¼ cup/65 g coarse sea salt

12 large basil leaves

16 green and golden zucchini/courgettes

½ cup/120 ml avocado oil

¼ cup/60 ml Champagne vinegar

10 zucchini/courgette flowers, stamens removed

cracked black pepper

oil, for brushing the grate

SERVES 6

Preheat the oven to 250°F (120°C) Gas ½.

Pulse together the salt and basil in a food processor, then spread the mixture out on a baking sheet. Bake in the preheated oven for 30 minutes until dry. Pour into a sterilized glass jar with a tight-fitting lid and set aside. (Any unused basil salt will keep for 2 weeks stored this way.)

Slice the zucchini/courgettes in half lengthways (or quarter them if they are large) and lay on a baking sheet. Whisk together the oil and vinegar and season with salt and pepper. Pour this over the zucchini and toss to make sure they are well covered.

Heat the grill/barbecue to medium–high. Brush the grate with oil.

Grill the zucchini for 3–4 minutes on each side until they are slightly charred and golden brown, then plate. Place the zucchini flowers on the grill and cook for about a minute on each side, then add to the zucchini.

Sprinkle with the basil salt and cracked black pepper and serve.

HEIRLOOM TOMATO & BLACK GARLIC *galette*

In August, when the farmers' market is at its best, you will see stands decked with bejeweled tomatoes of every type and size. From big fat rosy red tomatoes to dark purple and brightly green striped ones, they all make a huge statement. Have fun with this galette and mix and match colors and varieties.

10 mixed heirloom tomatoes

10 heirloom cherry tomatoes

1 lb/450 g ready-made puff pastry

3 tablespoons chopped black garlic

a few sprigs of thyme

1 egg, beaten

coarse sea salt

extra virgin olive oil, for drizzling

SERVES 6–8

Preheat the oven to 425°F (220°C) Gas 7. Line a baking sheet with baking parchment.

Cut the tomatoes into thick slices and the cherry tomatoes in half (or leave these whole if you wish).

Fold out the pastry on the prepared baking sheet. Using a knife, score a ¼-inch/5-mm border on each side of the pastry (but take care not to cut all the way through the pastry).

Top the pastry with the tomatoes, leaving the border clear. Sprinkle the garlic over the tomatoes and top with the thyme sprigs.

Brush the edges of the pastry with the beaten egg, then bake in the preheated oven for 20 minutes until brown and crusty.

Remove from the oven, sprinkle with salt, and drizzle with olive oil.

Mexican GRILLED CORN

Grilled corn slathered in cream, cheese, and chiles/chillies and finished off with freshly squeezed limes are known as "elotes" in Mexico and sold as street food. Use the husk as a handle when eating. I like to buy dried whole peppers and grind as needed as this keeps the flavor fresh, but using pre-ground is good too.

1 cup/250 g Mexican Crema or crème fraîche

½ cup/125 g mayonnaise

1 jalapeño, seeded and finely diced

1 tablespoon chili/chilli powder, plus extra for garnishing

1½ cups/160 g Cotija cheese (or feta cheese, if you cannot find Cojita)

sea salt

6 corn cobs in the husk

3 tablespoons olive oil

small bunch of cilantro/coriander, finely chopped

6 lime wedges, quartered

oil, for brushing the grate

SERVES 6

Heat the grill/barbecue to medium–high. Brush the grate with oil.

Place the crema, mayonnaise, jalapeño, chili/chilli powder, and half the cheese in a medium-sized bowl and mix together. Season with salt.

Peel the corn husks back and twist to make a handle. Brush the corn with the olive oil and place on the grill. Cook for about 10–12 minutes, turning every 3–4 minutes, until the corn is golden and caramelized.

When the corn is ready, generously brush the crema mixture over the kernels. Sprinkle with remaining cheese and cilantro/coriander and finish with a dusting of chili/chilli powder. Serve with the lime wedges to squeeze over.

Pickled strawberries & grape
BURRATA TARTINES

On my weekend visits to the farmers' market I always over-buy, especially in summer when the stalls are weighed down with plump, juicy fruits and berries. I either roast the excess or pickle it. I like to serve the burrata torn open with the fruit pickles and grilled bread on a big wooden board along with chilled wines. Dinner in itself.

loaf of rustic bread, sliced

olive oil

1 lb/450 g burrata

salt and freshly ground black pepper

flowering herbs, to garnish (optional)

FOR THE PICKLED STRAWBERRIES

24 strawberries, plus some leaves (optional)

1 cup/250 ml white balsamic vinegar

2 tablespoons kosher salt

2 tablespoons white sugar

1 tablespoon pink peppercorns

FOR THE PICKLED GRAPES

2 cups/5½ oz red grapes

1 cup/250 ml apple cider vinegar

1 tablespoon turbinado (or light brown) sugar

1 teaspoon kosher salt

1 red chile/chilli

SERVES 6–8

To make the pickled strawberries, pack them, and the leaves if using, in a sterilized jar with a tight-fitting lid. Place the vinegar, salt, sugar, and peppercorns in a pan with ¼ cup/60 ml water and bring to the boil over a medium–high heat. Cook for 3 minutes, then pour over the strawberries. Set aside to cool, then place the lid on tightly and refrigerate overnight.

To make the pickled grapes, pack the grapes into a sterilized jar with a tight-fitting lid. Place the vinegar, sugar, and salt in a pan with ¼ cup/60 ml water and bring to the boil over a medium high heat. Cook for 3 minutes, then pour over the grapes and add the red chile/chilli. Set aside to cool, then place the lid on tightly and refrigerate overnight.

Heat the grill/barbecue to medium–high.

Brush the sliced bread on both sides liberally with olive oil. Place on the grill and toast each side for about 2 minutes until golden brown and slightly charred.

Spread each piece of bread with burrata and top with the pickled strawberries and grapes. Season with salt and pepper, and garnish with fresh flowering herbs, if using.

Grilled TOMATO CAPRESE

Making your own ricotta is a breeze and absolutely delicious. The same goes for pesto—try this and you won't buy readymade again. This salad is perfect for a summer lunch, served with grilled breads and chilled rosé.

2 lb/900 g cherry tomatoes (about 6 branches)

basil leaves, for garnishing

oil, for brushing the grate

FOR THE RICOTTA

8 cups/1.9 litres whole milk

1 cup/250 ml heavy/double cream

⅓ cup/80 ml organic white distilled vinegar or freshly squeezed lemon juice

FOR THE PESTO

2 cups/100 g fresh basil leaves

½ cup/35 g freshly grated Parmesan cheese

½ cup/55 g chopped almonds

2 garlic cloves, minced

½ cup/125 ml extra virgin olive oil

1 tablespoon freshly squeezed lemon juice

salt and freshly ground black pepper

SERVES 6–8

To make the ricotta, pour the milk and cream into a large pan and place over a medium heat. Place a candy thermometer on the side of the pan and heat to 190°F (88°C).

Remove the pan from the heat and add the vinegar or lemon juice. Using a wooden spoon, stir the mixture very slowly a few times, then cover with a kitchen towel and set aside for 1 hour.

Line a strainer/sieve with cheesecloth/muslin and place over a bowl large enough to catch the whey. Gently pour the ricotta curds into the cheesecloth and let drain for 45 minutes. Place the ricotta in a glass storage container and season with salt and pepper, then cover and refrigerate.

To make the pesto, place the basil, cheese, almonds, and garlic in the bowl of a food processor and pulse a couple of times. With the motor running, pour in the olive oil in a steady stream. Add the lemon juice and season with salt and pepper. Pulse a few times to combine, then pour into a glass storage container.

Heat the grill/barbecue to medium–high. Brush the grate with oil.

Place the tomatoes on the grill and cook for about 4 minutes until they are bursting open and charred.

To serve, spoon the ricotta onto a platter and top with the grilled tomatoes, then drizzle with the pesto and garnish with the basil.

Store the remaining pesto in the fridge for another use. It will keep for up to a week.

ROASTED CAULIFLOWER
& red walnut Romesco

Red walnuts are so pretty—when you crack open the shells a dark red walnut falls out. You can substitute regular walnuts if you can't source the red ones. Make the sauce ahead of time, then all you have to do is roast the cauliflower. You can also cut the cauliflower into thick slices and brush with olive oil before grilling.

1 medium head of cauliflower

¼ cup/60 ml white wine

1 tablespoon salted capers

2 tablespoons fresh oregano leaves

extra virgin olive oil, for drizzling

sumac, for sprinkling

FOR THE ROMESCO SAUCE

1 cup/125 g red walnuts, or regular walnuts

2 cups/300 g heirloom cherry tomatoes

4 large garlic cloves, smashed

1 red (bell) pepper, quartered

¼ cup/60 ml olive oil, plus 2 tablespoons

2 teaspoons harissa (store-bought or see page 43)

1 tablespoon freshly squeezed lemon juice

sea salt and cracked black pepper

SERVES 4–6

Preheat the oven to 425°F (220°C) Gas 7.

To make the sauce, place the walnuts in a small cast-iron pan and roast over a medium heat for 5 minutes, then set aside.

Toss the tomatoes, garlic, and bell pepper with ¼ cup/60 ml of the olive oil, then tip onto a baking sheet and season with black pepper. Roast in the preheated oven for 20–25 minutes until charred. Remove from the oven and cool for 5 minutes.

Place the roasted vegetables in a food processor along with the remaining 2 tablespoons of oil, the harissa, and lemon juice and pulse until you have a thick, slightly chunky sauce. Season with salt and pepper and set aside. This can be made one day ahead and stored in the fridge.

Place the cauliflower in a Dutch oven/casserole dish, pour in the wine, then sprinkle with the capers and oregano leaves. Drizzle with olive oil, season with cracked black pepper, and place the lid on. Roast in the oven (also at 425°F (220°C) Gas 7) for 40 minutes, then remove the lid and continue to cook for another 15 minutes until cooked. You can check the doneness by inserting a sharp knife into the cauliflower.

Serve sprinkled with sumac and with the Romesco sauce on the side.

Squash blossom & corn QUESADILLAS

Just like tacos, quesadillas are served all over California. Normally a large tortilla is laid flat and filled with cheese, then folded over to seal. However, I like to make mine with two small tortillas in the style of a sandwich—that way, the filling gets melted and has a lovely charred crispiness to it.

12 corn or flour tortillas

1 cup/100 g shredded/grated Monterey Jack or Cheddar cheese

2 cups/350 g fresh corn kernels

1 zucchini/courgette, thinly sliced

12 zucchini/courgette blossoms, stamens removed and torn

1 cup/115 g queso fresco cheese

sea salt and cracked black pepper

TO SERVE
cilantro/coriander leaves, lime wedges, and hot sauces

SERVES 6

Heat the grill/barbecue to medium-high. Place a griddle or cast iron pan on top and heat until smoking.

Place six tortillas on a work surface. Sprinkle each tortilla with the shredded cheese, then top with the corn kernels and sliced zucchini/courgette.

Sprinkle with the torn zucchini blossoms and a little of the queso fresco (reserve some of the queso fresco for sprinkling on top of the cooked quesadillas).

Season with salt and pepper, then top with the remaining tortillas, pressing them down firmly to make a sandwich.

Place the quesadillas on the hot griddle and cook for 3–4 minutes, then flip them over using a wide spatula. Continue to cook for another 2–3 minutes until the cheese has melted and the quesadillas are golden and charred.

Plate the tortillas and cut into quarters. Sprinkle with the remaining queso fresco and cilantro/coriander and serve with lime wedges for squeezing and hot sauces.

DESSERTS

Vin Santo
GRILLED PEACHES

Peach season never lasts long enough for me as I adore plump, ripe, sweet, juicy peaches. I cut them up and toss them into salads, make ice cream and tarts with them, and eat them just as they are with good cheese. Here the peaches are soaked in Vin Santo, then grilled over mesquite embers until charred and caramelized. Enjoy with a small glass of Vin Santo.

4 medium ripe, firm peaches

8 tablespoons honey or honeycomb

1 bottle of Vin Santo

1 tablespoon finely chopped fresh sage

crème fraîche or sour cream, to serve

oil, for brushing the grate

SERVES 4

Heat the grill/barbecue to medium–high. Brush the grate with oil.

Cut the peaches in half and remove the stones. Lay the peaches cut-side down on the grill and cook for 3–4 minutes, then turn them over using a pair of tongs.

Place a tablespoon of honey or honeycomb in the center of each peach half, then fill with Vin Santo. Sprinkle the peach halves with the chopped sage. Cook for another 5 minutes until caramelized and slightly charred.

Serve with crème fraîche or sour cream and a small glass of Vin Santo.

MATCHA ICE CREAM
with black sesame praline

Delicious green tea ice cream with sweet crunchy sesame praline is a feast for the eyes! Matcha is green tea that has been ground into a powder which dissolves quickly in either hot or cold water to make a refreshing drink. Add it to cake mixtures and smoothies, or sprinkle over ceviche.

2 cups/500 ml whole milk

2 tablespoons powdered matcha green tea

1 cup/250 ml heavy/double cream

¾ cup/150 g cane sugar

6 egg yolks

FOR THE PRALINE

1 tablespoon toasted sesame oil

1½ cups/300 g cane sugar

½ cup/70 g black sesame seeds

SERVES 6–8

In a small bowl whisk together ⅓ cup/80 ml of the milk and the matcha powder and let sit for 5 minutes.

Pour the remaining milk into a saucepan, whisk in the cream and matcha mix, and then cook over a medium heat until just below boiling point.

In a medium-sized bowl whisk together the sugar and egg yolks. Slowly pour in the hot milk, whisking continuously, then pour back into the saucepan. Stir over a low heat until the mixture is thick and coats the back of wooden spoon. Set aside to cool to room temperature, then place in the fridge for 4 hours.

Freeze the chilled custard in an ice cream maker according to the manufacturer's instructions. Store in an airtight container in the freezer until ready to use.

To make the praline, brush a baking sheet with the sesame oil and set aside. Place the sugar in a saucepan with ⅓ cup/80 ml water over a high heat and cook for 6–8 minutes until dark golden brown. Do not stir.

Pour evenly over the prepared baking sheet and sprinkle with the sesame seeds. Set aside to harden. Break into chunks and serve with scoops of the ice cream.

Roasted strawberry
& GINGER SEMIFREDDO

I like to roast the strawberries as this gives them a deep, lush, rich, and intense flavor, which bursts with summer sunshine. Use stem ginger to give a gentle tang to the custard. You can turn the semifreddo out onto a large plate and slice to serve or scoop into bowls—either way will give you a dramatic and eye-catching dessert.

20 strawberries (about 1 lb/ 450 g), quartered

½ cup/100 g cane sugar, plus 2 tablespoons

3 tablespoons finely chopped stem ginger

3 large (UK medium) whole eggs

2 large (UK medium) egg yolks

2 cups/500 g heavy/double whipping cream

SERVES 6–8

Preheat the oven to 425°F (220°C) Gas 7. Line a 10 x 4-inch/ 25 x 10-cm loaf pan with plastic wrap/clingfilm.

Place the strawberries, 2 tablespoons of sugar, and the ginger in a food processor and pulse into a chunky sauce. Pour the mixture into a ceramic baking dish and roast in the preheated oven for 20 minutes. Remove from the oven and cool (this can be made a day ahead if you wish).

In a heatproof bowl whisk together the eggs, yolks and remaining sugar until just blended, then place over a saucepan of simmering water. Using an electric hand mixer, beat for 4 minutes. Remove from the heat and continue to beat for another 4 minutes until the mixture is thick and frothy. Set aside.

Pour the cream into the bowl of an electric stand mixer and beat until soft peaks form. Fold in the custard mixture until combined.

Pour a third of the cooled strawberries into the prepared loaf pan and cover with a third of the custard mixture. Continue to layer twice more.

Place a piece of baking parchment on top of the semifreddo, then cover with foil and freeze for 6 hours until firm.

Spicy DARK CHOCOLATE & COCONUT POTS

These dark little chocolate pots are a dream to eat and a dream to make. This is a simple recipe that can be whisked up quickly and ahead of time, which leaves you more time with your guests. I use Ancho chili powder to add a little kick, but you can use any kind of spice to give it an extra flavor dimension.

12 oz/340 g bittersweet/extra dark chocolate, 70% cocoa solids, finely chopped

2 teaspoons ground Ancho chili/chilli powder

½ teaspoon ground cinnamon

2 x 14-oz/400-ml cans of coconut milk

chocolate shavings, to decorate

SERVES 6

Break up the chocolate and place in a large bowl. Add the chili/chilli powder and cinnamon.

In a medium-sized saucepan bring the coconut milk to the boil over a medium–high heat. Pour the hot milk over the chocolate and stir until it has completely melted.

Pour the chocolate mixture into six small bowls or ramekins. Cover and place in the fridge for about 1½ hours until set.

When ready to serve, remove from the fridge and grate a little chocolate over each pot.

SUMMER FRUIT
& amaretto cobbler

Cobblers are a favorite with everyone. Tinged with a little old-fashioned familiarity, they make the most wonderful summer desserts. Mix and match berries and stone fruit, or keep it simple with just one kind. Serve warm with lashings of ice cream. You can easily cook this on a barbecue—just set the pan over indirect heat and close the lid.

6 ripe firm nectarines

10 ripe (but still firm) apricots

1½ cups/150 g blueberries

1½ cups/150 g blackberries

⅔ cup/150 g coconut sugar

1 tablespoon cornstarch/cornflour

¼ cup/60 ml amaretto

4 tablespoons/60 g cold unsalted butter, cubed

1½ cups/210 g unbleached all-purpose/plain flour

1 tablespoon baking powder

4 tablespoons dark brown sugar

pinch of sea salt

1 cup/250 ml heavy/double whipping cream

¼ cup/30 g chopped almonds

vanilla ice cream, to serve

SERVES 6

Preheat the oven to 375°F (190°C) Gas 5 or heat the grill/barbecue to medium–high.

Cut the nectarines and apricots in half and remove the stones. Slice the fruit into ½-inch/1-cm thick wedges and place in a large ceramic bowl. Add the blueberries, blackberries, coconut sugar, cornstarch/cornflour, and half the amaretto and stir, making sure all the fruit is evenly coated. Set aside to marinate for 30 minutes.

Place the butter, flour, baking powder, 2 tablespoons of brown sugar, and salt in the bowl of a food processor and pulse until the mixture resembles breadcrumbs. With the motor running, add the remaining amaretto and cream and process until the mixture forms a dough.

Pour the fruit mixture into a 12-inch/30-cm cast-iron pan. Using a dessertspoon, drop spoonfuls of the cobbler mix on top of the fruit, then sprinkle with the remaining sugar and the chopped almonds.

Bake in the preheated oven for 30–35 minutes until the cobbler is golden brown and the fruit is bubbling. If using the grill, place the pan on indirect heat, close the lid, and cook for about 20 minutes.

Serve with vanilla ice cream.

GOATS' CHEESE ICE CREAM
with grilled honey figs

Fig season arrives at the height of summer when the days are long
and the sun is hot. This dessert was created after a morning visit
to the farmers' market, when I returned home with a box brimming
with ripe and juicy plump figs. Grilling the figs infuses them with
a wonderfully rich, charred caramel flavor.

4 egg yolks

2 tablespoons granulated sugar

**2 cups/500 ml goats' milk or
    whole milk**

**1 cup/250 ml heavy/double
    cream**

½ cup/125 ml honey

**8 oz/225 g goats' cheese, at
    room temperature, crumbled**

pinch of kosher salt

**10 ripe black figs, halved and
    stems removed**

½ teaspoon ground cardamom

oil, for brushing the grate

SERVES 6–8

Whisk together the egg yolks and sugar in a medium-sized bowl
and set aside.

Heat the milk, cream, and half of the honey in a saucepan over
a medium–high heat until just below boiling point. Slowly pour
the hot milk mixture over the eggs, whisking continuously, then
pour the mixture back into the saucepan. Continue to cook over
a low–medium heat, stirring continuously until the custard is
thick and coats the back of a wooden spoon.

Pour the custard into a blender, add the goats' cheese and salt, and
blend until smooth. Cover and cool in the fridge for 2–24 hours.

Freeze the custard in an ice cream maker according to the
manufacturer's instructions. Store in an airtight container in the
freezer until ready to serve.

Place the figs in a ceramic bowl, add the remaining honey and the
cardamom, and toss to coat the figs. Set aside for 30 minutes
to marinate.

Heat the grill/barbecue to medium–high. Brush the grate with oil.

Grill the figs for about 4 minutes on both sides until caramelized
and slightly charred. Return the cooked figs to the bowl that they
were marinating in so they can soak up any excess juices. Cover
and set aside.

To serve, scoop the ice cream into bowls and top with the
grilled figs.

Grilled BANANA BOATS

An old-fashioned dessert from the diner, cooked on the grill and transformed into a wonderful caramelized dessert. Top with coffee ice cream and dark chocolate sauce, sprinkle with nuts, and dig in.

7 oz/100 g bittersweet/dark chocolate, 72% cocoa solids

2 tablespoons maple syrup

2 tablespoons/30 g butter

¾ cup/180 ml heavy/double cream

pinch of ground cinnamon

pinch of salt

6 bananas

1 quart/1 litre coffee ice cream

1 cup/225 g candied pecans, crushed

oil, for brushing the grate

SERVES 6

Heat the grill/barbecue to medium–high. Brush the grate with oil.

To make the chocolate sauce, place the chocolate, maple syrup, butter, cream, cinnamon, and salt in a pan over a medium heat. Stir the mixture continuously until the chocolate has melted and you have a smooth sauce. Pour into a small pitcher/jug and set aside.

Place the unpeeled bananas on the grill and cook for 3–4 minutes, then turn them over and continue to cook for another 5 minutes until the skins are charred.

Remove the bananas from the grill. Using a sharp knife, make a slit in the peel from top to bottom and open out slightly. Top each banana with a scoop of ice cream, pour over some chocolate sauce, and sprinkle with the pecans.

GRILLED RUM-INFUSED PINEAPPLE
with coconut ice cream

The dark tones of Jamaican rum infuse the pineapple and add to the wonderful depth of this mouthwatering dessert. Sprinkle with lime sugar, top with coconut ice cream, and enjoy!

1 large ripe pineapple

¾ cup/180 ml Jamaican dark rum

¼ cup/60 ml maple syrup

½ cup/225 g coconut sugar

zest of 4 limes

1 quart/1 litre coconut ice cream

¼ cup/20 g toasted coconut flakes

oil, for brushing the grate

SERVES 6

Using a sharp knife, cut off the top and the bottom of the pineapple, then remove the skin. Cut the pineapple into thick slices and place in a large ceramic dish.

In a small bowl whisk together the rum, maple syrup, and half the coconut sugar and pour over the pineapple slices. Set aside to marinate for 20–30 minutes.

Mix the lime zest and remaining sugar together in a small bowl and set aside.

Heat the grill/barbecue to medium–high. Brush the grate with oil.

Remove the pineapple wedges from the marinade and place on the grill. Cook for 5 minutes until they are caramelized and slightly charred, then turn over and continue to cook for another 5 minutes.

Pour any remaining marinade into a small oven-safe pan and heat on the grill.

To serve, place a piece of pineapple on a plate, top with a scoop of coconut ice cream, sprinkle with a little lime sugar, and drizzle with a little of the remaining hot rum marinade.

BLACKBERRY & PISTACHIO CAKE
with lime syrup

You can dress this cake up by piling lots of fresh berries on top with a few blackberry leaves and a dusting of confectioners'/icing sugar or simply leave as is. I either serve it warm with homemade vanilla ice cream, or make it a day ahead, drizzle with zesty lime syrup, and let sit overnight for the flavors to meld, then serve with a large dollop of crème fraîche.

2 cups/260 g all-purpose/plain flour

1 tablespoon baking powder

½ cup plus 3 tablespoons/ 150 g unsalted butter, at room temperature, plus extra for greasing

1 cup/200 g superfine/caster sugar

3 large (UK medium) eggs, at room temperature

1 cup/225 g whole milk Greek yogurt

¼ cup/1 oz salted pistachios, finely ground

1 cup/100 g blackberries, roughly chopped

FOR THE SYRUP

1½ cups/300 g white granulated sugar

zest of 4 limes

1 cup/250 ml freshly squeezed lime juice (about 4 large limes)

SERVES 8–10

Preheat the oven to 350°F (175°C) Gas 4. Line the base of a 10-inch/ 25-cm cake pan with a removable base with baking parchment. Grease the base and sides with butter and set aside.

Sift the flour and baking powder together into a bowl and set aside.

In the bowl of a stand mixer fitted with a paddle, cream the butter and sugar for about 5 minutes until light and fluffy. Add the eggs one at a time and beat until smooth. Add the yogurt and continue to beat.

Reduce the speed and slowly add the flour mixture, beating until well combined. Add the pistachios and stir to completely mix. Remove the bowl from the stand mixer and stir in the blackberries with one or two turns of the spoon until just mixed—you don't want the batter to turn pink.

Pour into the prepared cake pan and bake in the preheated oven for 1 hour until golden brown and a thin skewer inserted into the center comes out clean.

Remove the cake from the oven and place on a wire rack. Pierce the top all over with a skewer and cool for 20 minutes. Keep the cake in the pan.

To make the syrup, place the sugar, zest, and lime juice in a small pan. Bring to the boil over a medium–high heat, stirring to dissolve the sugar. Cook for about 5 minutes until it becomes a light syrup. Drizzle the lime syrup over the cooled cake, then loosely cover and leave overnight.

Drunken FRUIT SALAD

This is not so much a recipe as an opportunity to use any and all of the fruits in season. Stone fruits work the best as they keep their shape over hot coals, but you can grill pretty much anything—mangoes, bananas, and cherries are also good. If you want to grill berries, it's best to thread them onto skewers as this makes them much easier to move on the grill. I make this recipe with aquavit but you could use lemon-infused vodka or limoncello too.

6 yellow nectarines

6 white nectarines

12 green plums or greengages

12 red plums

1 cup/250 ml aquavit, plus extra to serve in liqueur glasses

3 tablespoons coconut sugar

mascarpone, to serve

oil, for brushing the grate

SERVES 6–8

Cut the fruit in half and remove the stones. Place the fruit in a large bowl. Pour the aquavit over the fruit, sprinkle with sugar, and toss to coat. Cover and place in the fridge for an hour.

Remove the fruit from the fridge and bring to room temperature.

Heat the grill/barbecue to medium–high. Brush the grate with oil.

Place the fruit on the grill cut-side down and cook for about 3–4 minutes. Using tongs, turn the fruit over and continue to grill for another 4–5 minutes until caramelized and slightly charred.

Serve the fruit with mascarpone and a small glass of aquavit.

Chocolate chip COOKIES

Decadent dark chocolate cookies must be a pantry staple. I like
to sandwich homemade ice cream between them (see page 126)
or serve them crumbled over grilled fruits (see page 122).

2 cups/260 g all-purpose/plain flour

½ cup/40 g cocoa powder, plus extra for dusting

½ teaspoon baking powder

½ teaspoon baking soda/bicarbonate of soda

pinch of kosher salt

12 oz/340 g bittersweet/dark chocolate, 70% cocoa solids, finely chopped

¾ cup/170 g unsalted butter, at room temperature

1 cup/210 g dark brown sugar

1 large (UK medium) egg

MAKES 20

Preheat the oven to 350°F (175°C) Gas 4. Line three baking sheets with parchment paper.

Sift together the flour, cocoa powder, baking powder, baking soda/bicarbonate of soda, and salt and set aside.

Melt 4 oz/115 g of the chopped chocolate either in a bowl set over a saucepan of simmering water or in a microwave. Set aside to cool slightly.

In the bowl of a stand mixer fitted with the paddle attachment, cream together the butter and sugar on medium–high speed for about 4 minutes until light and fluffy. Beat in the egg until combined, then slowly pour in the cooled melted chocolate.

Reduce the speed to slow and add the flour mixture a little at a time until combined, scraping down the sides of the mixer bowl as needed. Remove the bowl from the stand and stir in the remaining chopped chocolate. Cover the bowl and refrigerate for 5 minutes.

Using a small 2-inch/5-cm ice cream scoop or large spoon, drop the dough onto the prepared baking sheets, spacing them 4 inches/10 cm apart.

With the palm of your hand, press the dough down into 3-inch/7.5-cm circles, approx. ½ inch/1 cm thick. Cover and place in the freezer for 10 minutes.

Bake in the preheated oven for 15 minutes, then remove to a cooling rack. When cool, dust with cocoa powder.

Bourbon raisin
ICE CREAM SANDWICHES

Velvety ice cream laced with rum-soaked raisins and sandwiched between decadent chocolate cookies is a great way for grown-ups to end a barbecue. My tip is to keep a supply of dried fruits soaked in liquor in the pantry—they make fabulous additions to ice creams and desserts.

1 cup/100 g raisins/sultanas, golden or dark or mixed

1 cup/250 ml bourbon

4 egg yolks

½ cup/100 g turbinado sugar

2 cups/500 ml whole milk

1 cup/250 ml heavy/double cream

pinch of kosher salt

1 quantity of Chocolate Chip Cookies (see page 125)

SERVES 10

Place the raisins in a bowl and cover with the bourbon. Set aside to soak for 6–24 hours until the raisins have plumped up.

Strain the raisins and reserve the bourbon, which should yield about ½ cup/125 ml depending on how long you soaked them for.

Whisk the egg yolks, sugar, and bourbon together in a medium-sized bowl and set aside.

Heat the milk and cream together in a saucepan over a medium–high heat until just below boiling point. Slowly pour the hot milk over the egg mixture, whisking continuously, then pour the mixture back into the saucepan.

Continue to cook over a low–medium heat, stirring continuously, until the custard is thick and coats the back of wooden spoon.

Cover and cool in the fridge for 4 hours, then freeze the custard in an ice cream maker according to the manufacturer's instructions. When the desired consistency is reached, add the raisins for 2–3 turns of the paddle.

To make the ice cream sandwiches, lay ten cookies on a baking sheet and top with a scoop of ice cream. Top with remaining cookies and gently press together to make a sandwich. Individually wrap the sandwiches in plastic wrap/clingfilm and store in the freezer until ready to eat.

GRILLED DOUGHNUT S'MORES
with chile chocolate sauce

An all-out extravaganza of caramelized sugar, s'mores are one of those desserts that have no rules. Have fun by wrapping the marshmallows up in doughnuts, then toasting them and dunking them in a wonderful spice-infused chocolate sauce. Instead of doughnuts, you could also use cronuts or cookies.

7 oz/100 g bittersweet/dark chocolate, 72% cocoa solids

2 tablespoons maple syrup

2 teaspoons butter

¾ cup/180 ml heavy/double cream

1½ teaspoons ground cinnamon

½ teaspoon ancho chili/chilli powder

½ teaspoon smoked paprika

24 marshmallows

6 doughnuts, cut in half horizontally

oil, for brushing the grate

SERVES 6

To make the chocolate sauce, break up the chocolate and place in a medium-sized pan along with the maple syrup, butter, cream, cinnamon, chili/chilli powder, and paprika. Stirring continuously, cook over a low–medium heat until the chocolate has melted and you have a smooth sauce. Set aside.

Line a baking sheet with half of the the doughnut halves. Place four marshmallows on these, then top with the other halves. Press gently together to sandwich them together.

Heat the grill/barbecue to medium–high. Brush the grate with oil.

Lay the doughnuts on the grill and cook for about 1 minute on each side until brown and slightly charred.

Serve with the warm chocolate sauce for either drizzling or dunking.

Grilled PEACH MELBA

This is such a ubiquitous British dessert, invented at the Savoy Hotel in London by Escoffier to celebrate the Australian soprano Nellie Melba. He poached the peaches, but here they are cooked on a hot grill to release all their sweetness. Make life easy and pick a really good local artisanal vanilla ice cream.

6 medium, ripe but firm peaches

¼ cup/60 ml orange blossom honey

2 tablespoons turbinado sugar

1 pint/350 g fresh raspberries

¼ cup/60 g superfine/caster sugar

1 teaspoon freshly squeezed lemon juice

a few drops of rosewater

1 quart/1 litre good-quality vanilla ice cream

edible flowers, to decorate (optional)

oil, for brushing the grate

SERVES 6

Cut the peaches in half, discard the stones, and place cut-side up in a ceramic dish. Drizzle with the honey and sprinkle with the turbinado sugar and set aside.

Place the raspberries, superfine/caster sugar, and lemon juice in a blender and process to a smooth sauce. Stir in a few drops of rosewater and pour into a pitcher/jug.

Heat the grill/barbecue to medium–high. Brush the grate with oil.

Lay the peaches cut-side down on the grill and cook for 3–4 minutes until they are caramelized and slightly charred. Turn them over and continue to cook for another 3–4 minutes.

For each person, place two peach halves on a plate and top with a scoop of vanilla ice cream. Drizzle with the raspberry sauce and serve, decorated with edible flowers if you wish.

DRINKS

Pisco SOURS

The Pisco Sour originates in Lima and it could be considered Peru's national drink. Pisco—a spirit distilled from grapes—has a bright, lively flavor with grape aromatics. Invest in a good Pisco as it makes all the difference. Mixed with lime, it makes a really nice cocktail to be sipped slowly as the sun goes down.

ice cubes

½ cup/120 ml Pisco

¼ cup/60 ml freshly squeezed lime juice (Key limes if possible)

2 egg whites

3 tablespoons simple syrup (see page 145)

dash of angostura bitters

lime wheels, to garnish

MAKES 2

Fill a cocktail shaker with ice and pour in the Pisco, lime juice, egg whites, and simple syrup. Shake vigorously and strain into two glasses.

Top with a dash of angostura bitters and garnish with lime wheels.

APEROL *Spritz*

The Aperol Spritzs has a season and that is summer. It is a fun drink that is not too powerful and very refreshing. I like to dress it up by adding flowering herbs from the garden.

crushed ice
1 bottle of Prosecco
1 bottle of Aperol
club soda
1 tangerine, cut into quarters
flowering herbs, such as rosemary or basil, or flowers such as lavender, pansies, or honeysuckle, to decorate

MAKES 4

Fill four wine glasses with crushed ice.

Pour the Prosecco nearly three-quarters of the way up the glass, then add the Aperol (the ratio is three parts Prosecco to two parts Aperol). Add just a splash of club soda.

Squeeze the tangerine quarters into the glasses and decorate with flowering herbs or flowers.

APRICOT & BASIL *Mimosas*

This is a wonderful weekend brunch drink—light and fizzy with a herbal aromatics from the basil. Make the apricot and basil purée ahead of time (store it in the fridge for up to 24 hours) and when guests arrive all you have to do is add the chilled Champagne.

½ cup/120 ml simple syrup (see page 145)
4 basil leaves
8 very ripe apricots, pitted/ stoned
1 bottle of chilled Champagne

SERVES 4

In a small saucepan bring the simple syrup and basil to the boil over a medium-high heat. Remove the pan from the heat and let the syrup cool, allowing the basil to infuse. When cold, remove the basil.

Place the apricots and cooled simple syrup in a blender and process until smooth.

To make the mimosas, pour the apricot purée a quarter of the way up a chilled Champagne flute. Top up with the chilled Champagne and serve.

CUCUMBER *Martini*

I always feel healthy (and a little less guilty) sipping on one of these, although there is nothing wrong with a dirty martini with blue cheese-stuffed olives at the end of a hard week either...

1 Persian cucumber, peeled and chopped

2 tablespoons simple syrup (see page 145)

6 mint leaves

1 tablespoon freshly squeezed lemon juice

ice cubes

¼ cup/60 ml vodka

fennel flowers, to decorate (optional)

SERVES 2

Place the cucumber, simple syrup, mint leaves, and lemon juice in a blender and process until smooth.

Fill a cocktail shaker with ice and pour in the cucumber mix, along with the vodka. Shake vigorously and pour into chilled glasses, then decorate with fennel flowers, if using.

Bobbie's FIZZ

This is such a wonderful way to finish a meal. Tangy kumquat sorbet floating in icy Prosecco—it tastes even better than it looks. Serve in vintage coupe glasses for evening elegance and in small tumblers for a casual barbecue.

24 kumquats, tops trimmed
2 cups/400 g white sugar
1 tablespoon freshly squeezed lemon juice
pinch of sea salt
1 bottle of Prosecco, chilled
edible flowers, to garnish (optional)

SERVES 6

Place the kumquats in a medium-sized pan and cover with water. Bring to the boil over a high heat, then drain. Repeat the procedure twice more—this will reduce the bitterness of the peel. Place the drained kumquats in a blender.

Bring the sugar and 2 cups/500 ml water to the boil in a pan over a medium–high heat, stirring to dissolve the sugar. Reduce the heat to a simmer and cook for 5 minutes until the sugar has completely dissolved. Set aside to cool slightly.

Pour the sugar syrup into a blender with the kumquats and add the lemon juice and salt. Purée until smooth. Cover and set aside to cool, then refrigerate for 2 hours.

Freeze the mixture in an ice cream maker according to the manufacturer's instructions. Store in an airtight container in the freezer until ready to use.

To serve, add a scoop of sorbet to each glass and pour the Prosecco over the top. Garnish with flowers, if using.

The CAPRI

Campari brings such a refreshing herbal tone to any cocktail and it doesn't disappoint here. You can use tangerines, oranges, kumquats, or mandarins in this cocktail—it's a fun way to drink round the year with whatever is in season.

2 tangerines

¼ cup/60 ml Hendrick's gin

¼ cup/60 ml Campari

1 tablespoon freshly squeezed lemon juice

2 cups/450 g ice cubes

lavender sprigs, to garnish (optional)

FOR THE SIMPLE SYRUP

1 cup/200 g white sugar

SERVES 4

To make the simple syrup, place the sugar and 1 cup/250 ml water in a saucepan and bring to the boil over a medium–high heat. Reduce the heat and simmer until the sugar has dissolved. Remove from the heat and cool. This makes approx. 1 cup/250 ml. Store in a jar with a lid in the fridge.

Place the unpeeled tangerines, gin, Campari, lemon juice, and ¼ cup/60 ml simple syrup in a blender along with the ice cubes. Process until smooth.

Pour into chilled glasses and garnish with lavender sprigs, if using.

WATERMELON MARGARITAS
with Tajín-salted rims

Look out for the yellow watermelons with exotic names such as "Moon and Stars" or "Yellow Doll." They look exactly the same as the pink-fleshed melons but are a little sweeter. They make the most gorgeous colored margaritas, especially when rimmed with Chilerito Chamoy hot sauce and Tajín-spiced salt.

2 tablespoons Chilerito Chamoy hot sauce

¼ teaspoon Tajín seasoning

1 tablespoon coarse sea salt

½ cup/120 ml tequila blanco

2 cups/300 g yellow watermelon chunks

small bunch of mint

¼ cup/60 ml simple syrup (see page 145)

2 cups/450 g crushed ice

zest and freshly squeezed juice of 1 lime

MAKES 2

Pour the hot sauce onto a small plate. On another small plate, mix together the Tajín and salt.

Dip the rims of the glasses first into the hot sauce, then into the salt mix and set aside.

Pour the tequila into a blender and add the watermelon, four sprigs of mint, simple syrup, ice, and lime zest and juice into a blender and process until smooth.

Pour into the salted glasses and garnish with a mint sprig.

Spiced iced almond
HORCHATA FLOATS

These floats are a really fun way to end a big cookout. They are refreshing and not too heavy, and I like to serve them as a dessert. Make it for the kids too, but leave the rum out.

1 cup/140 g raw almonds

2 tablespoons brown sugar

1 teaspoon ground cinnamon, plus extra to garnish

½ cup/125 ml dark rum

crushed ice

vanilla ice cream, or a flavor of your choice

SERVES 4

Soak the almonds in water for 6–24 hours.

Strain the almonds and place in a blender with 2 cups/500 ml water. Add the sugar, cinnamon, and rum and blend until smooth. Pour into a tall pitcher/jug filled with ice.

Fill four tall glasses with crushed ice and pour in the horchata, leaving a space of 1 inch/2.5 cm at the rim. Top with a scoop of ice cream and dust with a little cinnamon. Serve immediately.

Summer SANGRIA

Make a large pitcher of sangria and sit back and relax. There isn't really a definitive recipe for sangria as you can add any kind of fruit, fresh or grilled, and top with wine and a splash of brandy. In summertime when the sun is high in the sky, lighter bright wines, such as rosé, are best used. Night-time sangrias, however, can use bolder reds. This is one drink that you should have fun making with seasonal fruits.

1 yellow peach
1 white peach
2 plums
1 orange, unpeeled
12 strawberries
½ cup/50 g blueberries
2 x 750-ml bottles of rosé wine
½ cup/120 ml brandy
¼ cup/60 ml simple syrup (see page 145)

MAKES 1 LARGE PITCHER

Cut the peaches and plums in half, remove the stones, and chop the fruit into 1-inch/2.5-cm chunks. Cut the orange into 1-inch/2.5-cm chunks. Slice the strawberries and place all the cut fruit, along with the blueberries, in a large pitcher and fill with crushed ice.

Pour in the rosé, brandy, and simple syrup and stir. Cover and refrigerate until ready to serve.

Grilled pineapple
PIÑA COLADA

This is a taste of the Caribbean with a wonderful rich caramel flavor provided by the grilled pineapple. Make these when you are having a party and friends are gathered around the grill. Finish with a dusting of freshly grated nutmeg.

½ pineapple, peeled

4 pineapple spears, to garnish

½ cup/120 ml simple syrup (see page 145)

½ cup/120 ml dark rum

½ cup/120 ml coconut cream

2 cups/450 g ice cubes

freshly grated nutmeg, to sprinkle

oil, for brushing the grate

SERVES 4

Heat the grill/barbecue to medium–high. Brush the grate with oil.

Place the pineapple half and the pineapple spears on the hot grill and cook until they are caramelized and slightly charred. Remove from the grill and roughly chop the pineapple half. Set the pineapple spears aside for the garnish.

Place the chopped pineapple, simple syrup, rum, and coconut cream in a blender along with the ice cubes and blend until smooth.

Pour into chilled glasses and garnish with the grilled pineapple spears. Dust with a little nutmeg and serve.

The NEGRONI

This gorgeous cocktail brings back memories of Italian vacations. I like to garnish it with different citrus slices, such as tangerines, blood oranges, or mandarins, depending on the season. If you wish, make it into a longer drink by topping off with some chilled Prosecco. Salute!

¼ cup/60 ml **freshly squeezed orange juice**
¼ cup/60 ml **Campari**
¼ cup/60 ml **Hendrick's gin**
¼ cup/60 ml **sweet vermouth**
ice cubes
orange slices, to garnish

SERVES 2

Pour the orange juice, Campari, gin, and vermouth into a cocktail shaker filled with ice.

Shake and strain into two chilled cocktail glasses. Garnish with orange slices and serve.

Infused VODKAS

I make infused vodkas and keep them in the freezer. They make a wonderful after-dinner digestif. I flavor them with all sorts of fruits, herbs, and chiles/chillies and as they sit in the freezer, the flavor intensifies. They are fun to bring to the table at the end of the meal when you are serving an ice-cold sorbet and let your guests choose a flavor to pour over. There are no rules with this recipe, except use good-quality vodka.

4 tangerines
2 lemons
fennel flowers
dried chiles/chillies
pink peppercorns
2 bottles of good-quality vodka
4 empty wine bottles

Sterilize the wine bottles by washing in hot soapy water or run through a hot cycle in the dishwasher.

Slice the tangerines and lemons into pieces small enough to fit into the bottles.

This is where you get to have fun and mix and match the ingredients and place them in the bottles. You can use a mixture of tangerines and chiles/chillies, lemons with fennel flowers, or just use a single ingredient, such as pink peppercorns, for each bottle.

Once you have filled the bottles with the ingredients, top them up with the vodka, then seal. Place in the freezer until ready to use.

Lemon & rosemary TISANE

Tisanes are a wonderful pick-me-up on a hot afternoon. Infused herbal and botanical drinks are a fun way to mix and match herbs from your garden. Sweeten with floral honey and drink iced or warm.

1 sprig of fresh rosemary
peel of 1 lemon
honey, to sweeten (optional)

Place the rosemary sprig and lemon peel in a teapot and cover with boiling water. Steep for 5 minutes, then serve with honey to sweeten if desired.

SERVES 2

INDEX

aïoli 62
almonds: charred Treviso salad 73
  pesto 94
  spiced iced almond horchata floats
    149
Amaretto: summer fruit & Amaretto
  cobbler 111
anchovies: charred Treviso salad 73
Aperol spritz 137
apricot & basil mimosas 137
aquavit: drunken fruit salad 122
avocados: fish tacos with avocado
    crema 34
  grilled avocados with Mescal & lime
    dressing 77
  poké bowls 37

bananas: grilled banana boats 115
basil: pesto 94
beef: classic cheeseburger 66
  grilled steaks with grilled tomatillo
    salsa verde 58
  Korean grilled skirt steak 57
beets/beetroots: jicama, apple &
  fennel slaw 81
black sesame praline 104
blackberry & pistachio cake 121
blue corn tacos 54
Bobbie's Fizz 142
bourbon raisin ice cream sandwiches
  126
brandy: summer sangria 150
branzini in a salt crust 16
bread: pickled strawberries & grape
    burrata tartines 93
  prosciutto & fig grilled flatbreads 65
burgers: classic cheeseburger 66
  lamb smash burgers 62
butter: garlic & chili butter 25
  nori seaweed butter 25
  wasabi butter 25
buttermilk: Cajun fried chicken 44

Cajun fried chicken 44
cake, blackberry & pistachio 121
Campari: The Capri 145
  The Negroni 154
caramel: black sesame praline 104
cauliflower: roasted cauliflower & red
  walnut romesco 97
cedar plank salmon 12
Champagne: apricot & basil mimosas
  137
cheese: classic cheeseburger 66
  goats' cheese ice cream 112
  grilled pizza with oysters &
    Parmesan cream 33
  grilled tomato caprese 94
  Mexican grilled corn 90

ouzo watermelon salad 74
pesto 94
pickled strawberries & grape
    burrata tartines 93
prosciutto & fig grilled flatbreads 65
roasted stuffed tomatoes 78
squash blossom & corn quesadillas
  98
chicken: Cajun fried chicken 44
  grilled harissa chicken kabobs 43
  sriracha & lime grilled chicken wings
    40
chickpeas: hummus 61
chicory: charred Treviso salad 73
chiles/chillies: chile chocolate sauce
  129
  clam steamers with Calabrian chiles
    30
  crispy pork belly blue corn tacos 54
  garlic & chili butter 25
  garlic chile shrimp 26
  grilled pizza with oysters &
    Parmesan cream 33
  harissa 43
  jerk pork chops 50
  piri piri Cornish game hens 47
  smoky honey chipotle ribs 53
chocolate: chile chocolate sauce 129
  chocolate chip cookies 125
  grilled banana boats 115
  spicy dark chocolate & coconut pots
    108
chorizo: clam steamers with Calabrian
    chiles 30
  paella on the grill 22
cilantro/coriander: smoky honey
  chipotle ribs 53
citrus-honey dipping sauce 47
clam steamers with Calabrian chiles 30
cobbler, summer fruit & Amaretto 111
coconut cream: grilled pineapple piña
  colada 153
coconut ice cream, grilled rum
  pineapple with 118
coconut milk: coconut & lime shrimp
    skewers 29
  spicy dark chocolate & coconut pots
    108
cookies, chocolate chip 125
coriander see cilantro
corn: Mexican grilled corn 90
  squash blossom & corn quesadillas
    98
Cornish game hens, piri piri 47
courgettes see zucchini
cucumber: cucumber Martini 141
  pickles 66
curry: coconut & lime shrimp skewers
  29

dates, grilled lamb with North African
  spices & 61

dipping sauce, citrus-honey 47
doughnut s'mores 129
drinks: Aperol spritz 137
  apricot & basil mimosas 137
  Bobbie's Fizz 142
  The Capri 145
  cucumber Martini 141
  grilled pineapple piña colada 153
  infused vodkas 157
  lemon & rosemary tisane 157
  The Negroni 154
  Pisco Sours 134
  spiced iced almond horchata floats
    149
  summer sangria 150
  watermelon margaritas 146
drunken fruit salad 122

fennel: jicama, apple & fennel slaw 81
fig jam: smoky honey chipotle ribs 53
figs: grilled honey figs 112
  prosciutto & fig grilled flatbreads 65
fish tacos with avocado crema 34
flatbreads, prosciutto & fig grilled 65
fruit: drunken fruit salad 122
  summer fruit & Amaretto cobbler 111
  summer sangria 150

galette, heirloom tomato & black garlic
  86
garlic: aïoli 62
  garlic & chili butter 25
  garlic chile shrimp 26
gazpacho cups, grilled heirloom 82
gin: The Capri 145
  The Negroni 154
ginger: roasted strawberry & ginger
  semifreddo 107
goats' cheese ice cream 112
grapes, pickled 93

harissa chicken kabobs 43
heirloom tomato & black garlic galette
  86
honey: grilled honey figs 112
  smoky honey chipotle ribs 53
hummus 61

ice cream: bourbon raisin ice cream
    sandwiches 126
  goats' cheese ice cream 112
  grilled banana boats 115
  grilled peach Melba 130
  grilled rum pineapple with coconut
    ice cream 118
  matcha ice cream 104
  roasted strawberry & ginger
    semifreddo 107

jerk pork chops 50
jicama, apple & fennel slaw 81

kabobs see skewers

Korean grilled skirt steak 57
kumquats: Bobbie's Fizz 142

lamb: grilled lamb with North African
    spices & dates 61
    lamb smash burgers 62
lemon: vine-leaf grilled trout 15
    lemon & rosemary tisane 157
limes: blackberry & pistachio cake
    with lime syrup 121
    coconut & lime shrimp skewers 29
    Pisco Sours 134
    sriracha & lime grilled chicken wings
    40
lobster: grilled lobsters with flavored
    butters 25

mango salsa 50
margaritas, watermelon 146
marshmallows: grilled doughnut
    s'mores 129
Martini, cucumber 141
matcha ice cream 104
Mexican grilled corn 90
mimosas, apricot & basil 137
mussels: paella on the grill 22

The Negroni 154
noodles, spicy peanut 70
nori seaweed butter 25

olives: aïoli 62
    ouzo watermelon salad 74
    roasted stuffed tomatoes 78
orange juice: The Negroni 154
ouzo watermelon salad 74
oysters: grilled pizza with oysters &
    Parmesan cream 33

paella on the grill 22
peaches: grilled peach Melba 130
    Vin Santo grilled peaches 103
peanut butter: spicy peanut noodles 70
pecans: grilled banana boats 115
peppers (bell): cedar plank salmon 12
    grilled heirloom gazpacho cups 82
    harissa 43
    spicy grilled salmon collar 19
pesto 94
pickles 66
    pickled grapes 93
    pickled strawberries 93
pineapple: grilled pineapple piña
    colada 153
    grilled rum-infused pineapple 118
piri piri Cornish game hens 47
Pisco Sours 134
pistachios: blackberry & pistachio
    cake 121
pizza with oysters & Parmesan cream
    33
plantains, grilled 50

poké bowls 37
pork: crispy pork belly blue corn tacos
    54
    smoky honey chipotle ribs 53
praline, black sesame 104
prawns see shrimp
prosciutto & fig grilled flatbreads 65
Prosecco: Aperol spritz 137
    Bobbie's Fizz 142

quesadillas, squash blossom & corn 98

raisins: bourbon raisin ice cream
    sandwiches 126
raspberries: grilled peach Melba 130
rice: paella on the grill 22
    poké bowls 37
ricotta: grilled tomato caprese 94
romesco sauce, red walnut 97
rum: grilled pineapple piña colada 153
    grilled rum-infused pineapple with
    coconut ice cream 118
    spiced iced almond horchata floats
    149

sake: cedar plank salmon 12
salads: charred Treviso salad 73
    jicama, apple & fennel slaw 81
    ouzo watermelon salad 74
salmon: cedar plank salmon 12
    spicy grilled salmon collar 19
salsas: grilled tomatillo salsa verde 58
    mango salsa 50
salt crust, branzini in 16
sangria, summer 150
sea bass see branzini
seaweed: nori seaweed butter 25
semifreddo, roasted strawberry &
    ginger 107
sesame seeds: black sesame praline
    104
shrimp/prawns: coconut & lime shrimp
    skewers 29
    garlic chile shrimp 26
    paella on the grill 22
skewers: coconut & lime shrimp
    skewers 29
    grilled harissa chicken kabobs 43
slaw: jicama, apple & fennel 81
s'mores, grilled doughnut 129
snapper/tilapia: fish tacos with
    avocado crema 34
spritz, Aperol 137
squash blossom & corn quesadillas
    98
sriracha & lime grilled chicken wings
    40
steak see beef
strawberries: pickled strawberries &
    grape burrata tartines 93
    roasted strawberry & ginger

semifreddo 107
summer fruit & Amaretto cobbler 111
summer sangria 150

tacos: crispy pork belly blue corn
    tacos 54
    fish tacos with avocado crema 34
tangerines: The Capri 145
    citrus-honey dipping sauce 47
    infused vodkas 157
tartines: pickled strawberries & grape
    burrata 93
tequila: watermelon margaritas 146
tilapia see snapper
tisane, lemon & rosemary 157
tomatillo salsa verde 58
tomatoes: clam steamers 30
    grilled heirloom gazpacho cups 82
    grilled tomato caprese 94
    heirloom tomato & black garlic
    galette 86
    paella on the grill 22
    red walnut romesco 97
    roasted stuffed tomatoes 78
tortillas: crispy pork belly blue corn
    tacos 54
    fish tacos with avocado crema 34
    squash blossom & corn quesadillas
    98
Treviso chicory: charred Treviso salad
    73
trout, vine-leaf grilled 15
tuna: poke bowls 37

vermouth: The Negroni 154
Vin Santo grilled peaches 103
vine leaves: vine-leaf grilled trout 15
vodka: cucumber Martini 141
    infused vodkas 157

walnuts: red walnut romesco 97
wasabi butter 25
watermelon: ouzo watermelon salad 74
    watermelon margaritas 146
wild rice: vine-leaf grilled trout 15
wine: Aperol spritz 137
    apricot & basil mimosas 137
    Bobbie's Fizz 142
    branzini in a salt crust 16
    clam steamers with Calabrian
    chiles 30
    paella on the grill 22
    summer sangria 150
    Vin Santo grilled peaches 103

zucchini/courgettes: grilled summer
    zucchini 85

ACKNOWLEDGMENTS

Summer rolled around and took us by the kind invitation of Todd Rubenstein to his ranch nestled in the rolling hills and farmland of Lompoc, California. Apple Creek Ranch sits between vineyards, a honey farm, and fields of organic produce as far as the eye can see. Thank you so much Todd for your gracious hospitality, taking us to feed the chickens, and letting me run into the fields at sunrise to harvest vegetables and flowers. The land is lovingly farmed by Andrew Gibson, of Sunrise Organics, who supplied all the vegetables, thank you. Erin Kunkel, thank you doesn't seem enough, you are so inspirational and shoot the most amazingly beautiful photographs. You did not put your camera down from dawn til dusk and the result is too heavenly for words. Gena Sigala, thank you so much for all that you touched. You brought style, beauty, and magic with all your props and styling. Thank you for hosting us and supplying our straw sun hats. A huge thank you goes to Connie Pikulas who tirelessly worked with me to cook up a storm and keep me straight! And for cooking our wrap dinner. Danny Hess, thank you for helping man the firepit and brewing iced coffee for our afternoon pick-me-up. Peter and Rebecca Work, of Ampelos Winery, Lompoc, for sharing their wonderful wines. As always, a huge thank you goes to Julia Charles and Leslie Harrington who asked me to write and style this book—it was a lot of fun being on location and cooking outside among the vines with the gentle ocean breezes coming over the hills. Thank you also to Miriam Catley and Gillian Haslam for their editing skills. Lastly but not leastly, a huge thank you and love go to Martin, my husband who champions me every day.

VALERIE AIKMAN-SMITH is a food stylist, chef, and author based in Los Angeles. Her work includes international assignments for magazines and she has cooked and styled her way through the Greek Islands, Paris, Mexico, Croatia, Scotland, and the U.S. Additionally, her work is seen in many commercials, print and advertising campaigns, as well as television and film. Valerie is the author of the cookbooks *Salt, Pepper, Pickled & Packed*, and *Smoke & Spice* for Ryland Peters & Small.

ERIN KUNKEL is an award-winning advertising and editorial photographer who works around the world and calls the foggy outer lands of San Francisco home. Known for being collaborative, optimistic, detail-oriented, and inspired, Erin and her team bring enthusiasm and experience to projects big and small. Erin is happiest exploring the world on shoots and adventures. She has also photographed *Smoke & Spice* and *Pickled & Packed* for Ryland Peters & Small.